BREAKING BARRIERS

BREAKING BARRIERS:

Blind Rites of Passage

The Extraordinary Stories of Uncommon People

Edited by
Frances Lief Neer

CREATIVE ARTS BOOK COMPANY
Berkeley • California

Copyright © 2000 by Frances Lief Neer

No part of this book may be reproduced in any manner without written permission from the publisher, except in brief quotations used in articles or reviews.

Breaking Barriers is published by Donald S. Ellis and distributed by Creative Arts Book Company

For Information contact:
Creative Arts Book Company
833 Bancroft Way
Berkeley, California 94710

ISBN 0-88739-299-7
Library of Congress Catalog Number 99-64932

Printed in the United States of America

For David Steinberg
journalist and gentle man
Sine qua non

My thanks to the storytellers,
without whom this book could never have been born.

TABLE OF CONTENTS

Preface xiii

Letter xvii

PART 1: OUR ELDERS

1 Folk Tales at my Grandma's Knee Told by a Native Son of California
   by DANIEL BREAULT 1
2 The Young Girl's Story,
   by MARY E. STEWART, Ph. D. 6
3 Loving Cody,
   by WANDA FORD 12
4 What I Do,
   by CODY BURNS 20
5 One More Problem to Solve,
   by SYLVIA SIMON 23
6 Eye Sore,
   by MARJORIE STERN 35
7 Legacies,
   by FRANCES LIEF NEER 45

PART 2: PARENTS & CHILDREN

8 Hearing Cassandra,
   by SUSAN PALMER 51

9 Jackson's Disease,
   by CHANA JACKSON 53

10 A Bag That's Full,
by NICHOLAS JACKSON 56
11 My Father,
by KATHY DEMPSEY 58
12 The Thom Family Story,
by JEFF THOM 63
13 The Story of My Life,
by KIMBERLY FOWELL 87
14 Two Sides of the Coin,
by PAMELA FOWELL 94

PART 3: SINGLES & SIGNIFICANT OTHERS

15 On Roads Not Taken,
by JAY WILLIAMS 107
16 Barriers or Building Blocks?,
by KATHY SEVEN WILLIAMS 112
17 Marching Forward,
by MIKE HOENIG 119
18 New Perspectives,
by LANCE DAWSON 129
19 Fading Sight,
by TANIA GREGORY 135
20 A Long Journey Home,
by CAROL HOWE 139
21 Moxie,
by KELLY WEISS 146
22 Looking to the Left,
by HENRY PASA 152
23 My Story,
by BRITT LINCOLN 155

24 Breaking the Barriers of Blindness,
   by ELENA STORER LASS 163
25 I See, Just in a Different Way,
   by RICHARD KING 166
26 Autobiography,
   by DESIRE VAIL 172
27 Seen Through Experience,
   by JEFFREY FRIEDLANDER 175

   Afterword: A Brief History of Blindness 185

   The Dick and Jane Primer of Common Eye Disorders ... 188

PREFACE

Questions to consider: How does a blind person dream? If a blind person had his sight restored, would he know what he was looking at? If you couldn't see, how would you know when a spoon was right-side up?

We are all many-layered individuals. No matter what we all have in common, each one of us also lives within a private world of experience. The stories collected in this book show how blind people adjust to everyday living in a sighted world, and how some sighted people have adjusted to living in the world of the blind. They also relate how blind people have broken through barriers and found their own individual paths to success. What carries blind people along is their own spirit, and what blind people can do often amazes and impresses the sighted.

Without a doubt, there are differences in how blind and sighted people perceive and understand their surroundings. Nevertheless, their basic needs and goals and desires are the same. We all rely on approval, love, and trust. All of our lives are structured around tradition and ritual. Rituals are overt actions in planned sequences, such as an engagement before a marriage, or eating your meat and vegetables before you get to dessert. Some rituals common to many of us include the first day of school, making new friends, religious confirmation, graduation, getting that first job, weddings, holiday celebrations, and parenthood. Rituals or rites of passage occur at all stages of life, from babyhood to preschool to college commencement to adulthood.

We need to consider rituals and rites of passage as ceremonies of commitment. Margaret Mead speaks of a cocoon of commitments within which we begin to make individual choices. Every day we accommodate, to varying degrees, the expectations of family, friends, and community. For example, immigrants accommodate as fast as they can to a new language, new foods, new social habits, different styles of clothing, schooling, and political systems, without entirely discarding their old ways.

Succeeding generations adopt the habits and language of the community, while within the nucleus of their own families they tend to keep up the old rituals. The everyday lives of people with special needs, in this case the blind, represent departures in habitual actions: how a person counts their money, uses a tape recorder instead of a memo pad, arranges clothing in their closet, organizes medicine and kitchen cabinets, chooses talking timepieces, goes to market, travels, and uses libraries or talking books. Blind people must teach sighted family and friends how they deal with life.

Breaking Barriers: Blind Rites of Passage is a collection of stories by extraordinary people, told in their own words, detailing their uncommon lives and their achievements in the face of adversity. They relate how touch, taste, smell and hearing compensate for sight loss. These stories demonstrate how people with visual impairments mold their environment and circumstance to meet their needs and achieve their goals. All of us, sighted or not, seek self-respect — from ourselves as well as others — and success in our private and public lives. Human needs and capacities are universal — to think, to talk, to share, to work; these are common conditions.

You might be amazed by what vision-impaired people can do. Could you imagine running a marathon without seeing the course? Could you ski or skydive or go horseback riding? Could you read a story with your fingers and your imagination, or fix a broken piano simply by touch? Could you cross a busy street without being able to see traffic, or take a public bus across a city? How well could you substitute facial expressions and body language for the tone of a voice or the touch of a hand?

Low vision people do all of these things, and more, as a

matter of course. The rites and customs of day-to-day living — of family, community, social and political life — are taken on. Visually impaired people mold and manipulate their needs in order to fit into the community, breaking barriers in spite of the frequently stiff odds against them. Adjustment and change are key in leading to action among people with visual impairment. They are are accustomed to rising above their limitations to meet the expectations of the people around them When they cannot, they must rely on family and friends for help.

These are indeed the stories of brave people who are confronting the odds and making the most of their situation. I have gathered these stories, including my own, in order to enlarge your understanding of people with special needs and their effect on all of us. Between these covers you will find stories that touch the heart and engage the mind. On these pages you will find a new alchemy of existence.

— Frances Lief Neer

January 5, 1999

Dear Frances:

Thank you so much for insisting that I write the enclosed story. I had a great time with it!

You are doing a wonderful thing to increase public awareness. Was there any one thing that convinced you to invest the time and energy to do something so constructive? I hear so many statements about how bad things are for blind people. How refreshing that someone is doing something to reach out to the general public to alter that situation.

I wonder what made you decide to present your case through the anecdotes of others. As a university employee, I am exposed to many journal articles from theorists who, when sharing thoughts or opinions of persons with disabilities, present them as case studies. How nice that you are letting people express things just as they see them! Have you received testimonials from sighted people who have benefitted from your books? I would be quite surprised if you have not.

Hope you don't mind my questions. As you can see, I am very much interested in your work. I respect you for being so obviously dedicated to this cause.

Kind Regards,
Mike Hoenig

PART 1
OUR ELDERS

FOLK TALES AT MY GRANDMA'S KNEE TOLD BY A NATIVE SON OF CALIFORNIA

by Daniel Breault

Note: I'm only telling this story because Mrs. Neer asked me to.

I was born in a foggy area of Northern California just outside Eureka, on a windy cliff called Bloomers Bluff. I must have been an awfully ugly infant, because from what I've been told, my father said, "Send him back, he's too ugly for me." But he was stuck with me.

I started walking when I was less than a year old, but shortly thereafter I succumbed to the first epidemic of what is now known as polio; it was called "infantile paralysis" in those days. It left me with feet that didn't seem to match and it made walking difficult, but I never let it slow me down any. As a toddler I'd crawl up onto my great grandma's lap and listen to the stories she told me about crossing the Plains in a covered wagon.

The year she came west was the same year as the Massacre of Utah, an event the Mormons still don't like to admit to today. Nevertheless, it's a matter of history. The Mormons dressed up like Indians, gathered together a few bonafide Indians, and massacred the travelers crossing the Plains in their wagon trains. As things turned out, though, my great grandma's wagon train got lucky. The guide they had hired to lead them across the Plains, a man named Southwind, hadn't heard about a shortcut the Mormons suggested to pioneers en route to California. Because of Southwind's ignorance, they escaped the massacre and arrived safely before winter. Great grandma had just gotten her household together when she heard that the Donner party was lost in a snowstorm in the Sierra Nevada, near what is known today as Donner Pass.

Great grandma crossed the Plains with her uncle, a man named Gallant Raines. Raines went on to open the first hotel in Mendocino County, the Occidental Hotel, which is still there today. The town of Raines was named after him.

When Great grandma first arrived in California, she settled in the town of Suisun, near San Francisco Bay. A much-feared Mexican bandit named Vasquez was scouring the countryside at the time, and one day he passed through Suisun and knocked at the door of my great grandma's house. He told her he was hungry and asked for some breakfast, which she served him. When he had finished eating, he told her he had no money, but he asked if she would accept a silk mantilla and comb in payment for his breakfast, which she did.

A few hours later Vasquez was captured and hanged, and after the hanging they cut off his head and pickled it in alcohol. To this day the head is kept at the Rosecrucian Museum in Santa Clara County. It's no longer shown to the public, but they still have the pickled head in their collection. My granddaughter now has the mantilla and comb, and the original redwood box in which Vasquez carried them.

After living in Suisun for several years, Great grandma wound up divorcing her husband and moving up to Eureka. There she met and married a Frenchman from Quebec named Doc Latrell, and she lived in Eureka until her death at one hundred. My own mother was Great grandma's second child. She had two brothers: Frank, who was killed in World War I, and William Joseph, who served in the United States Navy for nearly forty years and died in 1948.

My mother married and had four children. One, Salina Mary, died because the inept doctor Mother had at the time was drunk and neglected to tie the umbilical cord, so the infant bled to death.

My own life has not been quite so eventful. As I mentioned, I fell ill with polio in the summer of 1913. I had such a severe case that the federal government sent some of their doctors to examine me. They told my mother I might not live, but she didn't believe them, and being a very religious person, she took time out to pray. It seems her prayers were answered because here I am, still alive and kicking in my mid-eighties.

After I had recovered from my battle with polio, my mother started massaging my limbs. She bought an instrument—I don't remember what they called it—that produced a slight electric shock, and massaged my legs with it until I started walking again. I was almost five years old before she stopped the massage treatment. But polio left me without any muscles in the front part of my legs; I can't stand on my heels, and I have a stiff Achilles tendon. It never disturbed me too much other than when the kids made fun of me in school for the way I walked. After kicking the hell out of a few of them, they laid off of me, but I got into quite a few fights over it.

When I was still a boy we moved to the town of Alton. That's where I found out there was actually a sun in the sky. In Humboldt, the fog wouldn't lift until about noon, and it would come right back down again at about three o'clock, so we had about three hours of sunshine every day in the summertime. In fall and winter we had less than that.

Eventually our whole family moved further south, and it was on the way down to Oakland from Humboldt County that I saw my first Chinese person. He was standing in the doorway of a caboose on the railroad. I remember he was wearing a little black beanie hat, a full-length tunic (it looked like satin to me) that reached clear down to his ankles, and a pigtail halfway down his back. I called my sister, but she couldn't get up to see him because she had fainted from the heat. She had to wait until we got to Oakland to see Chinese people.

The trip was otherwise uneventful except for the night when the hotel where we were staying caught fire in the middle of the night. We had only slept half the night when suddenly we had to get up, get dressed, and wait the rest of the night for the train to take off again. We finally arrived in Oakland on July 3, 1919. I remember we spent the Fourth of July at the Shellmound Park on San Francisco Bay, which no one remembers anymore because it's nothing but a shopping center now. In those days, though, it was an amusement park where they had fireworks and a big to-do on the Fourth of July.

I suppose the next real thing of note in my life happened when I started school in Oakland. I got into a fight the first day of school. I hit the other boy top of the head and broke my thumb. In school was where I saw my first colored boy; African American you'd say these days. I had never seen a black person before because of an event called the Tong War in Eureka in 1898. A federal judge was killed, and in response the vigilantes ran all of the Chinese, Japanese, blacks—anybody who wasn't white—clear out of the county. They let one black man stay. He was married to an Indian woman named Minnie Moon, and they lived up in the mountains. They let him stay up there, so long as he never came into town.

For our first couple of months in Oakland we lived in a boarding house where my parents worked until my mother finally found us a home on Foothill Boulevard. We lived there for seven years before we moved to the house I still live in now. This house has withstood a lot, including three marriages—I'm on my third one now.

I went to Roosevelt High School in Oakland and graduated in 1929. One of the first jobs I had after I got out of high school was at a firm called Nell, Stratford & Kerr. One day while I was working there a young Jack Mormon (a lapsed Mormon) asked me if I knew anyone who was interested in going to college. I replied, "Yeah, I am." He said his parents paid for his tuition at Polytechnic College of Engineering, and he told me that for twenty-five dollars I could have his spot. So I gave him the money and enrolled in school. I was only able to go for two years, though, because the Depression hit and I was forced to drop out and go back to work.

I took about every kind of work you could think of just to get by, but eventually I settled down in the electronics department at Montgomery Ward. During the strike of 1940-41, I got a job with Mazwell Hardware, and I worked there until 1949, when I had to make a choice between taking photographs, which was my hobby, or working full-time for the Electricians Union—working for the Union just didn't leave much time to shoot pictures. I made my decision and worked for the Union for twenty-five years before retiring in 1973. After that, just to keep occupied, I taught jewelry-making in Oakland for about a dozen years as a volunteer. I had to give that up, though, when I went blind.

I started going to the blind center after that, and it irritated the hell out of me to hear some of the other people there say they didn't mind being blind. That to me is a doggone lie. I don't care if you're born blind—you resent it. At least I do. I resent it like hell because I've always worked with my hands and my eyes, and now I can't do those things. It's very frustrating. I'm just now accepting the fact that I have to ask other people for rides, ask people to do this and that for me. I can't read anymore, and I have to have someone read the newspaper to me if I want to hear the news. I don't know if I'll ever accept it fully. I accept the fact of it, but I just resent it all the time. I keep hoping maybe someone will find a cure—I don't think they ever will, but I keep hoping.

I'm not particularly proud of anything I've done in life, but I'm not ashamed of anything I've done, either. As far as I'm concerned, if someone doesn't like my gate, they don't have to swing on it.

THE YOUNG GIRL'S STORY

by Mary Stewart

The Preparation

My mother said, "He's old and has one eye."

Again she opened a world of questions for her young daughter: "How old?"

"One eye? How can he see with one eye?"

"Is there a hole where his eye should be?"

"How can an eye be made from glass?"

"Can he see through it?"

"If he only has one eye, what about the other?"

...and on and on. I was the grand inquisitor and new at learning about sight and its many variations.

He would be traveling a long way, and the adults would call him Major.

"Why?" I asked.

My grandfather had been in the Queen's Navy when he was younger and a British subject. When it came to him sleeping in my bedroom, there were no questions. I felt privileged that he would sleep in my room. I hurried to clean and rearrange it for him.

With my various welcoming tasks ahead, there were things I needed to take into account: he was old, he had traveled a long way, he had only one eye and poor vision in the other eye, and he walked with the help of a cane. I knew my mother loved him dearly.

My room had been painted light blue at my request when we first moved into our home in the country. My father had plastered the ceiling, creating an array of random designs that were like cloud shapes in the sky. I made a mental note to tell my grandfather about the designs. I practiced covering one eye and squinting the other while staring at the designs, so I knew he would be able to see them, too.

I had a desk and a set of bookshelves in my room that my father had made for me. These pieces of furniture were my domain. I took responsibility for cleaning and arranging all the items on my shelves and filling my desk drawers with the materials of my trade: pens, pencils, crayons, writing paper, construction paper, a diary, and other prized objects of my childhood.

The dresser and bed were my mother's domain. These pieces of furniture were part of my bedroom, but it was my mother who stripped and changed the sheets every week and lined my drawers with stacks of clean-smelling clothes. When it came to the matter of rearranging my bedroom, though, all of its contents were part of my realm. This was an ongoing, serious process that engaged me throughout my grade-school years.

My redesigned bedroom had to be perfect for my grandfather. I provided him easy access to space and hangers I had freed for him in my closet; to my bed, which I had stripped, and on which I had placed crisp, clean-smelling sheets and pillowcases; and to the desk, where I had placed my best writing pad, my favorite pens, some number-two pencils, and a pencil sharpener. On my bedside table I placed a clean crotcheted doily and my lamp with a new lightbulb in it, in addition to a glass of water and my favorite picture books. I figured he would be able to see big pictures with large writing.

Then, the pièce de résistance: the horse statues that were part of my growing collection. I dusted them and arranged them with maximum visibility in mind. With these many duties accomplished, I ran the vacuum cleaner across the carpet. My room was ready for him. I was excited.

The Visit

"When is he coming?"
"How will he get here?"
"Can I show him my room?"
"Can he sit beside me during dinner?"

Clearly, I was staking out my own territory early. When my grandfather arrived, he came through the front door. We never used the front door.

He wore a dark brown tweed suit with dark brown wingtip shoes and a white starched shirt with a muted tie that was tied with a thick Windsor knot. He was short, even shorter than my mom. His cane was made of dark wood with a white tip and a simply engraved silver handle. I figured my Uncle Bud had given it to him—the cane was Uncle Bud's style.

I couldn't figure out which of his eyes was made of glass—right, left...left, right. Mom told me not to stare. She also told me not to grab his arm, but rather to let him take my arm. I followed all of her instructions.

Mom had told him he would stay in my room on the first floor of our home. My father put his suitcase by my bed. The suitcase was made of textured brown leather and was covered with colorful stickers from many countries: my grandfather's history. I wanted to find out more about the stickers. Mom said, "Getting to know someone takes time." I paid attention to that.

I gave my grandfather a tour of my bedroom as if I were a museum docent. I pointed to the various conveniences I had designed for his comfort and provided suggestions on how best to use my room. For example, I thought he would like to look out the south window, where he could view the squirrels and chipmunks racing through a tall oak tree. He asked me to describe the view to him, explaining to me that he could not see as well as I could.

He was easy for me to see, though, because he stood only four feet nine inches, and I was three feet one inch. Height served as an equalizer in our family; every fraction of an inch counted. My need to see the eyes of loved ones started early in life. When my mother was pregnant with my brother Bruce I cried each time the doorbell rang. I could only be soothed when she raised me to her chest so that I could see her eyes.

I tried to put the matter of my grandfather's eyes in the back of my mind. I wanted to relate to his personailty rather than my fascination with his "lost eye" and the other eye with low vision. He acknowledged in turn each aspect of my bedroom tour in his crisp British accent. Politeness was important on the British side of my family. My mother and my uncles have all retained their accents.

My grandfather was soft and gentle, and he smelled sweet to me. When I inquired about his smell, he placed his finger to his lips as if binding us in a secret pact. He took a cigar from his inside jacket pocket, freed it from its cellophane wrapping, and sampled its aroma. He gently pulled the gold-colored paper ring from its circumference. He placed this ring on the middle finger of my left hand. It was pure magic for me. A ring from my grandfather on my left hand. How did he know I was a lefty?

We walked from my bedroom into the kitchen. I made sure I followed his rhythm and gait rather than rushing forward, as was my usual habit. As I entered the kitchen, which was a mere ten steps from my room, I realized I was out of breath. I was excited. If I could love my grandfather as my mother did, then maybe he would love me as well. I so wanted to be like my mother, to be loved as she was. What I didn't know at the time was that my grandfather would grow to love me, but not like my mother; he would love me as a granddaughter. I had never experienced this type of relationship. I suspect that there is no relationship like that of a grandfather to his granddaughter.

Major this... Major that... In my family, and particularly on my father's part, there was a great deal of respect and reverence for the Major. He had served in the Queen's Navy against Hitler. It was my grandfather who first told me about Hitler and the Holocaust. He told me stories about growing up in England, about his plants and trees there, and he taught me myths from the British Isles. He said that as his vision became more blurred, he used his memories of past vision to create stories for me.

The Last Story

By the last time my grandfather came to visit, he had taught me better methods of arranging my room for him, and I told him stories based on the things I now saw. The last visual story I told him—I can clearly remember—was on July 5, 1959. Every Fourth of July my family and I would go see the fireworks at the local country club. My grandfather, though, said he was tired and would just as soon sleep while we went to the celebration. I protested. I so wanted him to be with me; I begged him to come along.

Grandfather was ninety-six then, and as my mother explained, his "light was dimming," and he needed his rest. So I changed my strategy from trying to persuade him to come with us to promising him that I would be his eyes and ears and remember every detail of the fireworks so I could describe it to him the next morning. He told me he would like that very much.

While at the fireworks that night I took it all in, paying more attention than in previous years. I ran downstairs the next morning and met my grandfather in the kitchen, where he was chatting with my mother. I asked him to come out to the yard with me, and while we sat among the trees and plants, I told him a vivid story of fireworks, in all of its glorious detail: the colors, the rhythms, the designs, the response of the audience, as well as my thoughts and reactions. He told me it was the best story yet. After the story we sat in the sun and talked.

The next spring my grandfather died. I keep his memory alive inside me, though. I learned so much from him through his stories about how he navigated in the world after losing his eye during the war, and gradually losing the vision in his other eye. He taught me by example that he was not bitter or less of a man because of these changes, but rather greatly enriched. He passed on his way of living, coping, and adapting to life's vicissitudes to his young granddaughter, and these important lessons I keep with me to this day, thirty-eight years later.

LOVING CODY

by Wanda Ford

I was present when my grandson Cody was born. He was the third child of my daughter, Stephanie. When Cody was a month old, Stephanie and her three children moved in with us for a while, and it was then that I noticed Cody did not have normal eye movements.

When Cody was six weeks old I started talking to Stephanie about taking him to the doctor and asking about his eyes. My son (Cody's uncle) became angry with me, saying, "Just because you're a nurse you think there's something wrong with everybody."

"Be that as it may," I replied, "I think this needs checking into." So Stephanie and her husband, Bob, took Cody to the pediatrician, and she looked into his eyes so long that Stephanie finally asked, "Is Cody blind?" The doctor said, "I don't know, but I'm making arrangements for you to see an opthalmologist."

The next week we saw the opthalmologist, and Cody screamed and cried. When the exam was over the doctor said, "I can see to the middle part of the optic nerve, and it looks normal. His retina looks normal, too, but I don't believe there's any sight there." When we came home my son said that this was the worst thing that could ever happen, but I disagreed. Stephanie and I made arrangements to see a pediatric opthalmologist in San Francisco. The doctor arranged to check Cody into the hospital, and we were told that his retrogram was perfectly flat, that there was no sight at all. The doctor gave us a name for the condition later: nagstagnis.

Stephanie cried for two days, but once she got over the initial shock she became determined. "We have to get on with our lives," she said. So we just took care of Cody and loved him, and the other kids just adored him. He was such an absolutely beautiful child. Since we knew he was blind, we all made a lot of noise. He loved to be held, cuddled, and rocked, and he thrived on the hubbub. Cody's sister, Tiffany, was seven when he was born, and she would whistle as she carried him around. It was the only thing that would quiet him down and help him get to sleep.

At two months Cody started standing up on our knees, as babies do, and we would hold his arms while he jumped and jumped. To tell the truth, he's never stopped jumping in his seven-and-a-half years! We were told that many blind children are left to sit around on the floor, and consequently they don't develop their legs and hips properly. So we let Cody jump on everything except the bed, where he could fall off and hurt himself. My daughter even put mattresses on the floor of the living room for him.

Our doctor put in a call to the Blind Babies Foundation in San Francisco and sent a teacher to our home. Cody was three months old when the teacher first visited; she would bring noisy and tactile toys, and she came every month until Cody was five years old. The teacher worked for a blind attorney and knew a great deal about blindness and treatments for blind people. She taught us so much, and Cody was a fast learner.

When Cody was three, the teacher started him in with a white cane, which he absolutely hated (and still does). He has to use it at school to get to the bathroom by himself, but he refuses to use it at home. He recently learned how to dial a telephone. I remember the first night he learned to use the phone; he called me about fifteen times. These days he phones me, his grandpa, and his aunt and uncle quite a lot.

During Cody's fourth year, his teacher got us involved with the public school system. There was a mobile classroom at the school, and we would take Cody there three days a week. There were many handicapped children there, but he was the only blind child they had ever had. Cody just loved it. They had tactile toys and sang songs and played movement games. On nice days they would go out into the yard and play with tricycles and wagons.

When Cody turned five we took him to preschool at a nearby church. The first person he met was a teacher who had worked with blind adults for fifteen years. Every time she planned an activity for the sighted children, she would plan something equivalent for Cody. He loved that preschool, and he got along very well with the other children. At the end of the year, when it came time to decide where Cody should go next, one of the teachers suggested Head Start. But the Head Start classroom was so huge she feared Cody might feel lost there; she felt he needed a smaller, more structured environment. In the end we chose a school that was twenty-five miles away, but that offered a class for the visually impaired.

Boy, did we luck out! Cody's teacher, Kathy Dempsey, is a woman whose father was blind, so she was raised around blind people. Having no children of her own, she thinks of the kids at school as her family. When one of them has a birthday, she makes a big fuss over it and lets the kids make the birthday cake themselves with Braille measuring cups and spoons. The teacher and her aides give generous gifts to the kids, with Braille lables on the cards. It really makes the kids feel special.

My husband and I always take Cody to church and Sunday school with us. Cody loves to climb the steps, so when he got to be four-and-a-half I decided that if he could do that on his own, he could go to his Sunday school class by himself and become a little more independent. I would stand at the top of the stairs and put his hand on the railing, and he would go downstairs and take three left-hand turns, followed by one right. I waited until I heard his teacher say, "Well, hello Cody, come right in," and then I would go off to my own class. He thinks he's so grown up because he can do that.

These days Cody runs around our house, as well as his own house, without ever touching a wall or a door. Other kids ask, "How does he do that?" The truth is, I don't know. Maybe it's the sound waves bouncing off the walls. He goes all around the house and the garage, feeling everything. He calls this process "lookin' at it." He picks things up and moves them around. Not infrequently he'll ask, "Can I take this home? You don't need it anymore." So he now has half our kitchen utensils at his house.

Cody's teacher tells me he can do just about anything and has great potential. His dad is very mechanical, and ever since Cody was a small boy his dad has let him touch and feel the various things he was repairing. He talks to Cody while he works and explains things to him. This child can tell you where everything goes. When his dad gives him something that plugs in somewhere, he only has to teach Cody how to do it once, after which Cody knows how to do it forever. He'll tell you, "You're doing that wrong; it has to go this way."

It seems everywhere Cody goes he makes friends. He's a real happy fellow most of the time. He is also very good looking, tall and thin for his age, with blond hair and pretty hazel eyes. At church all the little girls hang around him and want his attention; several of them have volunteered to take him to children's church when the time comes. He's had one long-term friend his own age who comes over to visit with Cody. She's the only child who knows how to be a sighted guide. She and Cody have done so many imaginative things. They make up skits, which Cody sometimes records; they play them back and listen to them over and over.

When Cody was three years old he went to the first of many rodeos that the Monterey Sheriff's Posse holds for blind and visually impaired children. Ever since he was tiny, Cody hated fuzzy animals. He coined the word "doozit" to describe them. At the rodeo they let him touch one cowboy's horse, but Cody would absolutely not get on that horse. "It's a big doozit," he said, and everybody laughed. Eventually, though, he changed his mind and agreed to ride the horse. "It feels like Grandpa's boat going up and down on the lake," he exclaimed, which got a big laugh from the audience. After that he loved to ride, usually by himself with someone else leading. Now he goes to the rodeo every year.

Since Cody was very young, he's always wanted me to tell him stories. When he wants a story he says, "Tell 'bout, tell 'bout." He loves to hear stories about our cats. I've had eleven cats altogether, spanning thirty-eight years, and they're all buried out in the yard. Cody sees our yard as a giant cat cemetery, and he remembers all the details about each cat. I think he has what in a sighted person would be called a photographic memory, because he never forgets a detail.

One of Cody's favorite stories has to do with when he was hospitalized with pneumonia. At the time his favorite toys were kitchen utensils, and he would describe to the nurses all the utensils that were at his bedside. He would feel them and describe what they were. The nurses were all very impressed. They gave him loads of attention and tried to make life pleasant for him. Not being able to do much there, he talked a lot—one night until 4:00 a.m.—until I told him to stop talking, so then he started lifting his feet up and down instead.

Cody has been reading and writing Braille since kindergarten. Now, in the second grade, he has to copy all of his words five times a week. There are ten words to learn every week. He always waits until late to do his homework, by which time he is frequently tired and fussy. Sometimes I help him, kidding around with him and teasing him about who is the fastest Braille typist in the world. And when he starts making up sentences using his new words, the whole family joins in with the teasing. That seems to always put him in a good mood, and he finally finishes his homework. His teacher is very strict about homework. If the kids don't bring it in finished the next morning, they have to stay inside during morning recess until they get it done. If they still haven't finished, they have to stay in after lunch. She's helping them learn how important work is.

Cody has had a few little mishaps in his life. Once a boy who had minimal eyesight was supposed to be his sighted guide and take him to the bathroom. He ran Cody into a fence instead of turning him and Cody injured his forehead. Another time, when Cody was going by himself between buildings, he got off track, and even with his white cane he couldn't tell where he was. Eventually, though, a sighted boy offered to help him find his way.

He's had the feeling of being lost at least once. His dad and sister were watching him one day while he rode his bike up and down the driveway. But apparently they looked away at one point, and Cody turned right at the bottom of the driveway instead of stopping and going back up as he usually did. I guess he didn't turn around far enough, and he went all the way to the corner by accident. He got as far as the curb and knew he shouldn't go any farther, realizing he was lost.

He yelled, "Somebody help me, somebody help me," but no one could hear him because of all the traffic, and because he was in front of a vacant lot. He was hysterical by the time someone finally heard and his mother came to get him. He cried for an hour afterward because he was so lost and scared. We all tried to watch him more carefully after that incident, but he's getting more independent all the time. He loves to go into the garage by himself and examine everything in the toolbox and pretend he's driving the pickup. He turns everything on, although he's not quite so good at remembering to turn them off again.

There are lots of people in the community who enjoy doing things for Cody. There is a nearby florist who regularly takes kids on field trips to his pond. The pond is stocked with fish, and one of the florist's employees helps each blind child learn to fish, teaching them how to bait the hook and cast. Cody caught two fish last summer and was absolutely thrilled.

The Monterey County Symphony also has a very nice program. They divide the orchestra into four parts, each of which goes around to various schools in the area to teach kids about the instruments. Cody was thrilled when they showed him the percussion. Now he thinks he is going to be a drummer. He makes drum noises with his mouth all the time and keeps good rhythm.

There's a man in the neighboring town who built a railroad trestle and track all around his lot. He also built kid-sized cars for it, and when children come to visit he lets them sound the whistle and push the button that makes the train go. Then he takes them for a ride on the train. The kids love that.

Recently, Cody's class went to a pizza parlor in town, where the owner gave them a tour and let them feel everything that wasn't too hot to touch. Then he gave them each a piece of dough and various toppings and let them make their own pizza. They baked their pies, put their names on them, and what didn't get eaten at the restaurant they were allowed to bring home. That was a big thrill for Cody.

It's nearly the end of the school year now, and tomorrow each kid is going to bring money to school and the whole class will go out to a restaurant. This helps teach them how to eat in public, and they learn good table manners in the process. I don't know of any sighted class that gets to do as much as the blind and visually impaired class does. People are so wonderful to them, and they're always trying to think of something that will make their time a little brighter.

I would never have wished for my grandchild to be blind, but Cody has received so much unexpected help, and we've met such wonderful people through this blindness. I honestly didn't know such help was available. Sometimes we feel like the Lord lowered some of these people down from heaven. Because of Cody, our lives are infinitely more interesting. It really has been a wonderful thing to help this child grow up and to watch him and love him and be with him. We just love him to pieces.

WHAT I DO

by Cody Burns

I want to tell you about the fire station field trip we had today, okay? When we first got there we saw a fireman come down the stairs and slide down the pole. Then he put all his gear on, but the thing I liked best was the tank he wore like a backpack. If he stopped moving, a signal would go off that tells the other firemen he's hurt; maybe a beam hit him in the head and knocked him out or something. The next thing he did was turn the fire truck on and we saw the strobe lights. They ticked kind of like a clock. Then he started the truck up—it was kind of loud—and we saw the truck.

After leaving the fire station we crossed a busy street and went to Rosie's for lunch. I had some rice and beans and a burrito. Then we went to the library and played on the grass until our bus driver came. The bus is pretty interesting. I wish I could learn about the wheelchair ramp and see how to push the buttons to make the ramp go up and down. I wish I could see it. Maybe I should ask my bus driver tomorrow.

At school in the morning I do my calendar. On Mondays I do writing; I write CB for my initials. Then I do some reading. I go to recess, eat snacks, do my spelling, and write in my journal. Then I go to lunch and recess. In the afternoon I listen to tapes, then I have math and social studies. After that I pack up my backpack, and we go outside to physical education if there is any time, and then I go home. That's my day.

At recess I play ball sometimes. One time I bounced the ball back to myself. My friend Randy got a ball once and tried to shoot it into the basketball hoop we have. We don't really use it a lot, though. Sometimes people get hit on the head when the ball goes through the hoop. And you know, sometimes when they throw the ball it hits the shutters. One time a kid hit that shutter so hard we heard it all the way across the classroom. I thought it would make the shutters open and break all the little windows. I didn't want that to happen.

One time two mean kids came into the boys' bathroom when I was there. One of them took my cane, and I had to chase him all around the bathroom to get it back. Finally I got the cane and went back to class. I told my teacher about what happened, but she didn't know where the boy was who took my cane. But she finally found him and told him not to do that. I've never seen him since then.

My sister is kinda mean to me sometimes. She's kinda tough, like most sisters are. Sometimes she yells at me when she's mad. If she's really mad she'll hit me or pinch me. Sometimes I hit her back, but then she pinches my neck and I have to try and slap her away. My friend and I run away from her sometimes, and then she cries. We're not trying to be mean to her or anything, but when she's being mean to us we want to hide from her.

One time at school we flew a kite. It was kind of fun, I guess. And then one day on the bus we kinda got too loud. The bus driver got mad and turned the radio off. I was telling people to be quiet so he wouldn't get even madder. One time at school the teacher told me to put my head down. I almost had my head down the whole day. It was not fun. I didn't like it. I finally got to eat lunch.

One day at school I was supposed to be reading some rhymes, but I didn't want to read them. My teacher got really mad. This was the last straw, and I went to the office. I didn't go to time-out, but I did have to talk to the substitute principal. Then I went back and tried to do some math. And then you know what happened? I didn't want to do my math, either. My teacher sent a note home with a sad face. I didn't like that.

One time we went to Point Lobos and saw some trees. I

saw a caterpillar, too, I think. We heard some sea lions. Then we climbed some rocky steps and ate our lunch. After that we played around, and I got to play on some driftwood. I don't know anything else to tell you about, so I'll ask Grandma and see if she knows any more.

ONE MORE PROBLEM TO SOLVE

by Sylvia Simon

I'm a problem solver. Ever since I was a young girl, I've taken charge of situations, made decisions when others were immobilized, and looked after family members. Now, at age eighty-two, I'm confronting the most difficult challenge of my life: coping with failing vision.

Sixteen years ago, I was diagnosed with glaucoma and, more recently, with cystoid macular degeneration. I am legally blind in my right eye and have diminished vision in my left. I have had one cataract surgery, several laser surgeries, and a surgery to correct drooping eyelids—all to no avail. My vision has continued to decline. With the aid of a magnifying glass and bright light, I can read just enough to handle my personal bills, but it has been a while since I have been able to enjoy my favorite pastime: reading. Last year I suffered the biggest blow yet to my independence when I had to stop driving.

Until my vision problems began, I had minimal contact with doctors. Fifty years ago, long before it was fashionable, I studied about nutrition and alternative healing. I knew intuitively that, whenever possible, it was better to undertreat rather than overtreat a physical problem. When other mothers rushed their children to pediatricians every time they had the sniffles, I treated my children's colds by giving them fruit juice mixed with crushed vitamin C tablets. When I had problems with recurring cysts, I successfully treated them with hot compresses instead of going to the doctor to have them incised. And when I developed adult onset diabetes, I controlled it through diet and avoided taking insulin. My self-confidence in knowing my own body and how best to treat it, however, may have misled me when my vision began to fail.

I knew something about glaucoma, since my mother had the disease. Because of the strong hereditary component, I routinely had the pressure in my eyes checked by my optometrist. In 1982, when I was diagnosed with glaucoma, I contacted Dr. L, the opthalmologist who was then treating my mother. He had good credentials and had been in practice for several decades. Surely he would know what he was doing.

Dr. L prescribed eye drops to control the pressure in my eye. I didn't worry about the glaucoma too much because I trusted that if I faithfully used the drops the disease would be controlled. Later, when I developed cataracts, I didn't worry particularly about them, either. After all, cataract surgery had become a routine procedure. I knew many people who had cataracts removed, and none of them had any problems. I was confident that I was in good medical hands and that my condition was manageable.

Although I was aware that my vision was impaired, I was still able to drive, read, and live as I always had. It wasn't until after I had cataract surgery that I began to question the medical treatment I was receiving. Dr. L had a large office and a waiting room that was constantly crowded. A typical visit involved a long wait, an initial eye exam conducted by an assistant (usually a technician), followed by a rushed conversation with Dr. L, who concluded each visit by telling me to schedule another appointment in six months.

That seemed like a long interval between visits for someone with my condition, and I regularly found myself pestering Dr. L's receptionists to give me an appointment, complaining that my vision was declining. Finally the doctor agreed that the cataract in my stronger eye was ripe for surgery.

Instead of improving my vision, though, the surgery made it worse. My eye was badly inflamed, and now I was worried. I kept after Dr. L., telling him something wasn't right. In response to my complaints, he recommended laser surgery to treat the glaucoma in both eyes. That, too, failed. Since I am a borderline diabetic, I asked him whether I might have diabetic retinopathy. He dismissed the notion with a wave of his hand. I continued to see Dr. L, but I was beginning to lose confidence in him.

It was becoming evident that Dr. L was too busy to put much thought into my case, and I concluded that if I was going to get any help I would have to take responsibility for myself. I couldn't count on doctors to think about me. I had to do what I had always done in the past—take charge of the situation. With my magnifying glass in hand, I began reading up on opthalmologists in my area.

Because of my interest in alternative medicine, I generally preferred doctors who took a holistic approach to medical care. I found a young woman who impressed me with her positive attitude and warm personality. She told me that she knew of patients who had been cured of glaucoma by a procedure in which an injection was made directly into the eye. I thought to myself, "Well, Dr. L isn't helping me and my vision is worsening; what do I have to lose?"

Unfortunately, the new doctor's optimism was greater than her healing skills. In the process of injecting the drug, she ruptured some blood vessels, and the areas surrounding my eyes were black and blue for months. I sheepishly returned to Dr. L, who asked me what had happened. "Oh," I lied, "I bumped into a cabinet because I can't see where I'm going." Dr. L prescribed me some new drops in addition to the ones I was already taking, and for a while this brought the pressure in my eyes under control. He was baffled, however, by the swelling behind my eye. He told me he could do nothing more for me and suggested that I see a retinologist.

I continued to wonder if the swelling was somehow related to my diabetes. The first retinologist I consulted said it was possible the two were connected. Wanting a definitive answer, I consulted a second retinologist, who stated emphatically that I did not have diabetic retinopathy. Unlike Dr. L, who rarely took the initiative in recommending a new regimen, this doctor ordered more laser treatments and changed my medication. I was initially hopeful that he could help me. The new treatment did cure the inflammation, and it reduced the swelling in the backs of my eyes. It did not, however, improve my vision. It all turned out to be moot, however. Before I could decide whether I wanted to continue seeing this doctor, he dropped me, explaining that he no longer took patients covered by my HMO.

I was back to square one: I had to find a new opthalmologist and a new retinologist. I started my research again. One by one, I called the eye specialists listed in my HMO's handbook of providers. I wanted to know where they had studied, how long they had been in practice, and how old they were. After my experience with Dr. L, I preferred to see younger doctors who had been trained in the latest techniques and who still felt a sense of mission to help their patients.

The next opthalmologist met all my criteria, but our initial meeting could have been a scene out of a Woody Allen movie. He greeted me, walking toward me with a visible limp. In between taking notes on my medical history, he complained about his sore knee. Falling into my old role as helper, I asked him what the problem was. I signaled him to move his chair next to mine, and I applied acupressure to the painful spot. A week later, when I called his office, I asked him about his knee. "Oh," he said, "Thanks so much for your treatment. It's feeling much better."

I had my doubts about this doctor, but I also recognized that I had few options, given the limitations of my HMO coverage. I had run through all the opthalmologists in my area, and unless I was willing to pay out of pocket for medical care, I was limited to the providers on my HMO's list. It makes me angry that I don't have the right to choose my own doctors.

I had better luck in tracking down a new retinologist. When I learned that Dr. B had graduated from Washington University in St. Louis, which has a prestigious medical school, and that he was in his early forties, I made an appointment to see him. For the first time in all my encounters with eye specialists, I felt encouraged. Here was a doctor who did not seem rushed, who took an interest in me as a whole person, and who seemed determined to help me. My first visit lasted an astonishing four hours.

After taking a thorough case history and carefully examining my eyes, he ordered an angiogram. The test showed a swelling in the backs of both eyes. He told me to continue using the same eye drops until he got back in touch with me, and he was as good as his word. I didn't have to hound and pester his office to get a response. He promptly called me back and told me that he had called my opthalmologist to see how the two of them could work together to preserve my remaining vision. On the next visit, he was equally unhurried. For nearly an hour, he pored over the Physicians' Manual, reading aloud to me and my son the different possible medications and their side effects.

Dr. B withdrew the medication I had been taking for fourteen years and prescribed three new medicines. My eye pressure returned to normal, but the swelling behind my eyes remained unchanged. Dr. B thereupon recommended a more radical measure, and on my last visit he injected a solution directly into my eye. It is still too early to determine the results, but what seems clear is that I have finally found an eye doctor who has a heart as well as a mind. I was impressed that he called my opthalmologist without my having to ask him, that he follows up with his patients, and that he keeps experimenting with different medications and treatments. Also, unlike a lot of other doctors, he doesn't give up on his patients just because they are elderly.

Dr. B is an exceptional doctor, and I feel lucky to have found him. But what does it say about the state of medical treatment in this country that a concerned doctor should be an exception? In the end, his efforts may not make any difference. Maybe I waited too long to see a retinologist. Maybe nothing can be done to help my vision. Only time will tell. But at least now I have a doctor who genuinely wants to help me.

In the meantime, life goes on, and the truth is, it isn't easy. It is frustrating having to read with a big magnifying glass in my hand. I lose my place as I read, and I'm forever losing my papers as well. I seem to spend half my day looking for things, even though I'm probably better organized than most people. For many years I was a businesswoman, and I learned about organizing from my father. He had a successful business in Chicago sewing bridal veils. He trimmed the veils with beads, feathers, lace, and buckles, and everything had to be in its place so that he could easily find what he needed. All the decorations were stored in individual drawers and tagged with precise labels.

My father started to teach me the business because at the time my husband was out of work and we had two small children to raise. One day I was assisting my father in the shop as normal when two armed burglars barged in. One pulled a gun and ordered me to open the cash register. My father was in the back room sewing a bridal veil. He heard the commotion and ran into the storefront shouting, "What's going on?" His sudden appearance rattled the burglar and he fired the gun, killing my father.

His death left my brother and me in a state of shock and my mother totally bereft. She had never been able to take care of herself and was totally dependent on me and my father to look after her. Everyone thought I would have a nervous breakdown because I loved my father so much and because I had witnessed his murder. I knew I had to be strong, though, because I would have to take care of everyone, and that's exactly how it turned out. My brother was so devastated by our father's murder that he had a nervous breakdown, and I nursed him back to health. My mother, who was always very melodramatic, now had an actual tragedy to carry on about.

It wasn't practical for me to take over my father's business because I didn't have his talent for sewing. One day, as I was taking an inventory of supplies, I found notes in drawers that my father had written to remind himself where different trims were stored so that he could find them quickly. These notes were proof to me that my father was still at my side, watching over me. As I catalogued the items in his shop, I got the idea to start a mail-order costume jewelry business. The fact that I didn't know the first thing about costume jewelry didn't stop me. The idea had potential, and I decided to pursue it.

I made regular visits to the Art Institute in downtown Chicago to study the paintings and antique jewelry collections to get ideas for color schemes and designs. Inspired by the work of the great masters, I began designing bracelets, necklaces, and brooches. Soon I was ready to launch the business. I ordered a variety of stones so that customers could personalize my designs with the colors of their choice. My husband worked with me, and later my brother joined us as well. The business continued to expand, and at its height we advertised in thirty-five magazines. I was proud to have conceived and built a business that was lucrative enough to support my mother, my brother, and my family.

In 1978, I moved my mother from Chicago to my home in Berkeley, where she lived with me for ten years until her death at age ninety-two. I never really understood just how little she could see with her glaucoma, perhaps because she had always demanded so much care. My mother thrived on attention. At home she was self-centered and demanding; in public, she was a charmer who never lacked for an audience.

She loved to sing, and with her deep voice and repertoire of songs in Yiddish, Russian, Polish, and English, she quickly developed a fan club at the North Berkeley Senior Center.

She also loved to tell stories—the same ones again and again. Although she had emigrated to the United States from Russia when she was ten years old, she mangled the English language with hilarious malapropisms and her own invented vocabulary. My mother regarded herself as a star and me as her handmaiden.

Now that my own vision has failed, I feel guilty about the scoldings I used to give my mother. I didn't realize how bad her eyesight was, and I attributed her idiosyncratic behavior to her need to have others take care of her. Sometimes I'd walk into her room and find her watching a television that was a screen of snow. I thought she was just sitting there waiting for me to fix it.

"Why don't you adjust the screen?" I'd ask. "You can't see anything through all that snow.

"I can see," she would insist, "I can see."

Being neat and well-groomed was always very important to me, and I was embarassed when my mother would want to go out with big, bright circles of rouge on her cheeks. "You look like a clown," I'd say, wiping off the rouge with a hankerchief. "Why don't you use the magnifying mirror that I bought for you so you can see what you're doing?"

I accused her of being equally careless about her clothing. "How can you go out in public wearing such dirty clothes?" I'd ask when she would put on dresses with big grease spots before going to the senior center. Now I'm in the same boat my mother was in. Recently, a cousin who was visiting told me that my blouse was covered with spots. That was hard for me to hear because I have always been so careful about my appearance. Now, before I get dressed, I take my clothes over to a bright light and inspect them for spots, but the truth is I still miss half of them.

More than many women my age, I have always been self-reliant. From the time I was a young child, it was I who took care of my mother, rather than she of me. In addition, I took care of my husband, I took care of my brother when he needed help, and I took care of my children. In the 1970s, I was a participant in a program in Berkeley called SAGE. It was started by a remarkable woman, Gay Luce, who had the idea that she could help change negative attitudes about aging by introducing people sixty years and older to yoga, meditation, visualization, and self-care.

I have been interested in metaphysics since I was in my forties, so I felt at home with the spiritual aspect of the program. What I wasn't so good at was thinking about myself. Sometimes staff members met individually with participants. One man, Joe, used to check in with me to see how I was doing, whereupon I would recite a litany about how I was taking care of my mother, my husband, our house, our rentals, and helping out my adult children.

Joe would listen to my recitation, and then he'd ask, "And what about Sylvia? What's left for Sylvia?" I never took his questions seriously at the time because they were so foreign to me. It didn't occur to me to think about my own needs. I was the person who took care of everyone else, and that's all there was to it. If I took the time to do things for myself, who would do all the other things that had to be done for the family?

Ever since my husband died, I have managed my financial affairs on my own. But as my vision declined, it took me longer and longer to do the paperwork. My children and friends told me to hire a secretary, but I wouldn't hear of it. I insisted that the paperwork was too complicated and that no one else could handle it. Finally, last month, though, I reached my limit. Reading had become such a struggle that I was throwing out all but the most essential mail, and even then, I was spending hours at my desk trying to read my bills. I recognized that I could no longer handle the paperwork alone. It was time to hire a secretary.

I put an ad in the university newspaper. Because my hearing is also getting worse, I needed an assistant who was not only bright and capable, but who also spoke loudly and clearly. I interviewed several candidates and selected a lovely and intelligent student who conveniently lives within walking distance of my house. She comes over twice a week for two hours to read my mail to me and help me organize my papers. She's rewriting my address book in giant letters so that I can read the numbers, and just last week I asked her if she would spend part of her time reading aloud some of my favorite books. The arrangement has worked out well. I'm up to date on my bills and correspondence, and best of all, I enjoy this young woman's company. Bright and cheerful, she is a pleasure to be around.

So, little by little, I am learning to rely more on others. My son and his wife have been living with me for the past two years. They often drive me to doctor's appointments or take me shopping, but I don't want them to be my chauffeurs. Luckily, the city of Berkeley offers transportation services for the elderly and disabled. I use a door-to-door service to go to the doctor's office or shopping.

The service is not without its drawbacks, however. I have to make appointments for pickup a day in advance, so I can never do anything on the spur of the moment, and because the van picks up other people it often runs late. That's not bad when I'm at home, but it's a nuisance when I have to wait in front of the grocery store with my shopping bags. But what are my alternatives? I can't drive and I don't want to depend solely on my son and daughter-in-law. So I learn to wait. I learn to be patient.

When I was younger and living in Chicago, I studied with a teacher of metaphysics. She introduced me to the concept of being present in the moment and taking things one step at a time. One winter day we were talking in my living room. She looked out at the naked trees and said, "Some people look at those barren limbs and think the trees are dead. They're not dead; they're dormant. In the spring, they'll bloom again. The cycle of dormancy and renewal is true in nature and in all life." I have always remembered that, and whenever I feel depressed, I remind myself that I am in a dormant period—a time for me to be quiet, to reflect, to prepare for renewal.

My interest in metaphysics has sustained me through many of the difficulties I've experienced in my life. When I feel dispirited, I don't deny my depression; I don't feel I have to hide it. I have legitimate reasons to mourn my failing vision and the losses it brings. I used to love to drive around town, browse in stores, scout out new restaurants or, at the last minute, take in a movie. Now I'm denied those pleasures. I can't just pick up and go when I feel like it. I often feel isolated and lonely and have periods of depression.

Even in my darkest moments, though, I understand that my depression is temporary, that it will pass and I will keep going. I know I will never give in, and I will never give up. As bad as my vision is, I'm still in possession of my income, and I'm still generating income all by myself from stocks and rentals. It gives me a sense of power and satisfaction to know that I am still in control. One day I may have to give up those things, too. I don't look forward to it, but if it comes to that I know I'll find a way to deal with it.

What I still haven't figured out is what to do about my house. It's a big house with a substantial garden, and both require constant maintenance. I periodically feel overwhelmed by all the work I have to do to keep this property in shape and over the past five years, and I have more than once been on the brink of selling the house and moving to Santa Cruz, where my daughter and granddaughters live. "Come on down here where we can help you," they say. But they all have their own lives. My daughter has a full-time career, and my granddaughters like to travel, so I would still be on my own.

The biggest obstacle is finding a place where I fit, where I feel I belong. My daughter has looked at many houses and investigated various senior housing complexes, but none of them seems right for me. I've lived in this house for twenty-five years. How can I give up the home I love—a beautiful, organic living space—to go live in some plastic complex? That is my dilemna, or so I tell myself. Maybe the truth is that I can't find the right place because I'm just not ready to move.

So, for now, I do what I've always done. I wake up in the morning, do my exercises, fix my breakfast, and ask myself, "So, Sylvia, what do you have to take care of today?" Then I sit down at my desk and make a list of what needs to be done—just as I did yesterday, and just as I will do tomorrow. That's how life goes. You take care of one thing, and then you move on to the next. As long as I have breath, as long as my mind is clear, I will search for solutions because that is who I am: Sylvia, the problem solver.

EYE SORE

by Marjorie H. Stern

The only picture I have of myself as a baby shows a somewhat morose-looking child about a year old looking away from the camera. No one would have guessed from looking at me then that I was blind in my left eye. In fact, nobody—including me—knew it until years later. I guess in the post-World War I years no one tested childrens' eyes before they went to school. No one tested mine, anyway. The only indication that something was wrong were the frequent eye infections I contracted, including one that my aunt described as so severe my face was disfigured and swollen halfway down to my chin.

My mother died in a flu epidemic when I was four months old. Left in the care of my father and two brothers, ages two and six, I must have been an unappealing sight, since my eyes were often red, puffy, and sore. Babies are a lot of work even when they are healthy. I was, unfortunately, a problem.

My father had several sisters, all with big families of their own, and after a brief stint in which he hired a home nurse to take care of us, he gave up trying to keep us all together and parceled us out to these various aunts. My brothers were bundled off to our maternal grandmother two thousand miles away, and I had trials with three different aunts before ending up in a foster home. I feel certain my aunts' inability to take care of me stemmed from my baffling eye infections that no doctor could seem to diagnose.

Growing up in a foster home was not all that bad an experience for me. I was loved by my middle-aged Auntie and Uncle, and they had a teenage daughter I was a little sister to.

I had to learn to be quiet because they lived in an apartment building in Chicago. I was never disciplined too harshly, and I worked at my school lessons diligently.

When it came to physical activities, however, I was neither a graceful nor an agile child. One of the favorite activities among kids in my neighborhood was roller skating, but I could never keep up with my friends on the block. My Auntie would dutifully strap my skates on and set me out on the pavement, where the other kids all floated around without apparent difficulty. But over and over again I would fall, skin my knees, and end up sitting dejectedly on the sidewalk. The boy across the street would taunt: "So Fatty's learning how to skate!" It was humiliating.

Ice skating on the pond in the local park was all but impossible. I skittered and scattered, tipped over, and spent more time nursing an icy bottom than gliding over the ice. Once again I was cut out of the fun, and I would always welcome the spring thaw so I wouldn't have to embarass myself on the ice anymore. But once springtime arrived and all the kids would start riding their bicycles, the art of balancing on two wheels was beyond me.

One thing I did excel at was reading. It was something I could accomplish without relying on balance, and I could do it at my own pace. A book could be held close at hand, and it didn't demand any dexterity. I began to read in the silent movies at age four, still not realizing that I was seeing with just one eye.

The periodic infections in my left eye continued throughout my childhood. Sometimes they were just a case of pink eye, but often I would develop painful sties or full-blown bacterial infections where my eye would become flaming red and blisters would form around it. I was somehow able to keep up in school despite frequent enforced absences due to the infections. My infections worried my father, my foster parents—who solicitously nursed me—and my Aunt Ray, a well-to-do matron who patiently led me from doctor to doctor until my father remarried when I was twelve years old.

Much earlier, when I was only three, a doctor had come to our home to examine me, and he ended up performing an operation on my eye on the dining room table! I have no memory of these events, and my family kept no records or documentation of my eye trouble. In retrospect, I think this was because I had no mother to look after me.

On another occasion I remember taking a long trip from Chicago to Michigan to see a specialist. One eye doctor (we didn't know the proper titles of opthalmologist, optician, or optometrist in those days) prescribed cold baths in which I would be rubbed with coarse salt, presumably to increase my resistance to infection. I endured these treatments, diligently administered by my foster mother, but I didn't like them. I do remember that I enjoyed a generally better diet than others in the family. I enjoyed plenty of fresh-squeezed orange juice even though fresh fruit was hard to come by. In those days, only root vegetables and canned produce were readily available during the winter.

In elementary school, my poorest subjects were handwriting and art. Every night after supper, my Uncle would take me to the dining room table to practice the Palmer Method of handwriting. No one could understand why my handwriting was so misshapen and crabbed. I spent several years practicing the rounds and swoops of proper handwriting, but I never mastered the pristine script. Could it have been because I saw the lines differently than most people? My placement of letters was skewed because of the way my eyes viewed things, but no one ever thought to question why this was so. I was simply viewed as inept.

I excelled at anything that involved books and intellectual acumen, and I ended up graduating near the top of my class. Maybe it was the cock-eyed way I looked at the world, or maybe it was something about the medium itself, but I remember my otherwise proud sixth-grade teacher calling me aside at graduation time and saying, "Marjorie, you are good at everything you try, but stay away from art!"

Another bane of my existence in elementary school was glasses. My father belonged to a men's social club, and among his acquaintances there was an "eye doctor," who I now know was simply an optician. He would try lens after lens on me, asking, "Do you see better now?" Finally, he would fit my black-rimmed glasses with what he deemed to be the most promising lenses. I hated my owl-eyed look, and somewhere along the line I discarded the hated glasses completely. Years later I would learn that these exercises with the optician were a complete waste of time.

Junior and senior high school were an exciting prospect for me, partly due to the construction of a new school in my neighborhood, complete with a fully equipped gymnasium, showers, lockers, and an Olympic-sized swimming pool. In my high school, every student had to pass a swimming test in order to graduate. A problem that had dogged me during summer vacations at the beach was the fact that I didn't know how to swim. Now, with a beautiful new pool right in school, I could get instruction from my physical education teacher.

At first I was reticent. I had been frightened of the water as a child after being pushed off a pier into a lake. Compounding my fear was the fact that once I managed to get in the water I couldn't see where my arms and legs were. While my friends leapt excitedly into the pool and splashed off to the deep end, I was left behind with the younger kids. It was only after a patient and sympathetic teacher took a great deal of time with me that I was finally able to muster my courage and pass the beginner's test in school.

That wasn't the end of my troubles in the physical education department, though. While I was excelling in the classroom, making all kinds of new friends and singing my heart out in the glee club, my stock plummeted in sports. I was small for my age, and in any game that required using a ball I was a complete dud. It didn't matter if it was volleyball, softball, golf, tennis, or just plain catch. I couldn't catch a ball to save my life. Neither could I hit one, and consequently, no one wanted me on their team. I took to hiding behind the building in my green gym suit so I wouldn't have to bear the humiliation of not being picked.

Another form of aggravation involving a ball surfaced during my senior year. Someone had devised and instituted a proficiency test of physical skills that every student had to pass in order to graduate. Among them was an accuracy test in which students had to throw a ball at a bull's eye fastened to the gym wall. Needless to say, I failed hands down. Included in the same test were several climbing, somersaulting, and contorting exercises. I couldn't master these, either, and I had to endure the humiliation of an F in physical education on my report card.

After completing high school and college I settled into a good job as a stenographer with the National PTA. Oddly enough, given my vision-related problems, I discovered that I was unusually adept at picking out typos and mistakes in content. Because of my uncanny ability to catch printing and typing errors, I was designated as the final person to read the galleys of the various PTA publications prior to their going to press. I still retain this facility, even though to this day I only see with one eye.

In truth, I never felt that I suffered from a handicap, except of course for my high school experience in team sports. No teacher or PE instructor ever tested my eyes during my school years. In fact, I was constantly being told what beautiful eyes I had. It wasn't until I entered college at San Francisco State at the age of thirty-five that I learned I should never have anything to do with ball games on account of my eyesight. The PE department at San Francisco State gave its own physical examinations to determine which sport or activity a student should take in order to fulfill the graduation requirements. I was advised that only swimming and dancing were suitable for me.

Another attempt at fixing my errant eye occurred just before I was married at the age of twenty-one. My fiancée, wanting me to be the perfect bride, took me to the best-known opthalmologist in Chicago for a diagnosis of my perhaps beautiful but nearly sightless left eye. His opinion was that all the previous attempts at curing my condition with glasses had been misguided. He said the real reason I couldn't see was scar tissue clouding my cornea, probably caused by the infections I had suffered as a child. His solution was to cut several of the blood vessels feeding the scar tissue. Unfortunately, the procedure didn't improve my sight, and cornea transplants were either unheard of or too expensive to try at that time.

Sixteen married years passed before any more attempts were made to improve my vision. By this time my husband and I had moved to San Francisco and started a family. I had given birth to four children and I was a housemom. It was with the birth of my last child (a much-hoped-for girl after three boys) that the crisis occured. I was severely ill following the birth, and I remained in the hospital with a breast infection and high temperatures. Finally, I was able to take my daughter home, but the very next day I arose with an extremely inflamed left eye. My lifelong experience had taught me that this was a sure sign of trouble. I was examined that day by a specialist, who diagnosed my condition as an ulcerated cornea—a very serious infection.

The next six months were unadulterated hell for my husband and me. I was in a weakened condition with a new baby and three other children to take care of and little in the way of household help. I couldn't drive, but I was expected to regularly travel nearly twenty miles to a clinic in Oakland. My husband had to take off half a day from work to drive me to the clinic, where we would sit and wait for any free time the specialist might have. My left eye would then be dilated and treated with what I was led to believe was an experimental serum in drop form.

The dilation caused photo phobia, or fear of light, so I could—and eventually would—only sit in dark rooms. I isolated myself, refusing to go out into the daylight, and in time I developed a fear of seeing other people. My husband started hiring a Saturday night baby-sitter, insisting that I go out at least once a week. Making things even more difficult for me was the fact that I could not even see my new baby properly. I had no depth perception, so I couldn't tell whether a shape on the floor was a hole, a mound, or flat on the floor. I had to learn to see things all over again.

I grasped the railings when walking downstairs; I bumped into things; I had to be careful when using knives or other hand tools to make sure I was aiming at the proper object. After six months the doctor told me he could no longer keep my eye dilated, but when my eye returned to its normal state there was a new build-up of scar tissue that I was forever trying to see around. I was involved in a re-education in visual acuity. My depth perception was gone, and I couldn't see to sew, type, or do any work that required fine coordination. If people looked closely, they could see the scar tissue covering my eye. And to top it all off, I still didn't know what my little daughter really looked like.

Adjusting gradually to these conditions, I carried on tending the children at home. Eventually, though, I began going out one night a week to attend a parent cooperative nursery school class. Since I had so many children to put through nursery school I went to these classes for six years. One summer I organized a preschool children's art show at the California State Fair in Sacramento. We had a booth in the non-profit section of the fair, and in one of the nearby booths my husband found a display that included an eye test administered by a local optometry association. He dragged me over to it and insisted I take the test. I felt it was a pointless excercise, but to my astonishment the test showed that I had perfectly good peripheral vision in my bad eye. Unfortunately, this revelation did not lead to any immediate action.

It was several years later, when the new eye bank at U.C. San Francisco began looking for corneas on which to operate, that my husband again insisted that I be tested. This time the examination was the most thorough I had ever had. Once the results were in, the doctors offered to perform a cornea transplant on me as a teaching case (our finances allowed us to live comfortably, but we weren't able to afford the $8,000 cost of the operation in 1955). Since I was attending school part-time to earn a bachelor's degree, I scheduled the operation for the end of the semester.

At that time patients were advised to stay in the hospital for two full weeks, heads sandbagged and body immobilized to promote healing. I wrote a short article on the experience of undergoing the operation. It was performed under local anesthetic, but with the patient too drugged to care what was happening. The article was entitled "An Eye for an Eye." I remember sending it to my doctors to read, but it was never published.

For the first time in my life, at age thirty-five, the doctors were finally able to explain to me that the cause of my lifelong vision difficulties was a form of herpes virus that my eye had been exposed to in the birth canal. The virus now lived in the nerve of my eye, and during times of low resistance it leaped out and attacked my cornea, much as one might get a cold sore on the lips under similar conditions. The lips, however, are not as vulnerable as are the eyes.

The operation on my cornea, though not a total success, did result in a great improvement to my vision. My doctors explained to me that if an eye does not "see" by the time one is six years old, certain things necessary for the development of proper sight do not develop. Evidently this was the case with my bad eye. My cornea was clear, but it had been sewed on crooked during the operation, so my vision remained a bit skewed. My depth perception returned, though, and a year later I learned to drive without any problems; the State of

California permitted me drive with the sight perfect in only one eye. I was doing well in college, I could sew and type again, and I was very happy. At the age of forty I graduated from S.F. State and became a school teacher.

My restored sight lasted twenty-eight years, until one day shortly after my retirement I awoke to another flaming red eye. At the time I was living with my son's family in Washington, D.C., where I was a grandmother and child care provider. I rushed off to the clinic and was sent straightaway to the hospital, where a specialist delivered the unwelcome news that I had an ulcerated cornea. Both the news and the eye were painful, as we were all preparing to move back to California after the birth of a grandchild.

We went through with the move as planned even though my left eye was still inflamed, and I placed myself in the care of a specialist once we had settled in San Francisco. This time around I was alone in taking care of myself. The specialist was able to save my cornea, but again my sight changed and I had to learn how to see things yet one more time as my eye adjusted to the new medicine I was taking.

This dosing of my eye to keep the cornea clear was successful for twelve years, and then suddenly one day the cornea clouded over completely. For the next year I was completely blind in that eye. I would bump into people and things, both at home and in the street, and I had to be extremely cautious driving. Eventually my doctor operated, giving me yet another cornea transplant. This one was easier than the last. I only had to remain in the hospital for one day and I got up immediately to walk around. Yet again I had to learn to see—what color things were, what shape things were, what edges to avoid, how far away they were. I had to do this with everything, from the smallest tools and household implements to large items. Hadn't I done all this before?

I suppose most normal-sighted people take sight for granted until they reach middle age and discover they need glasses. Those of us who struggle with varying degrees of sightedness develop an awareness of what we cannot see and a timidity of new situations. Darkness poses an enormous problem as one loses the ability to see at night. A person with normal vision cannot imagine how black the darkness seems or how glare can affect an eye with a cataract, blurring one's vision and causing lights to grow large fuzzy halos.

Since my other eye—the normal one—also changes with age, life has become a transitory kaleidoscope of change and wonderment. Other eye conditions produce other visions. I can only speak for my own somewhat cock-eyed view of the world. I have managed to get along, and even excel in some areas, but I do not wish my condition on anyone else.

LEGACIES

by Frances Lief Neer

The day my son died I began a new life. This is not to say, mind you, that I sat in the wings waiting for Bill to pass on so that I could just be done with him; rather, life took on a richness after his death that he would have loved to be part of. Who would think that so much tragedy could lead to so much growth?

I mourned Bill's death before he died. We mourned together. Every day for six months we talked about who would take care of the family matters, the legalities, and—most importantly—who would take care of his daughter, Christine. Her mother was already gone, and none of Bill's friends could take her in. Finally, one day he put it to me: "You as an old person will have to bring up a young person."

Being "old" wasn't the problem per se. The problem (I saw it as a problem then) was the blindness that was coming over me like a slow, dark tidal wave. I could still do some cooking and use the telephone, but traveling, going to the market, and reading were all falling away along with my sight.

Here I was: seventy years old, losing both my son and my eyesight, faced with the care of my thirteen-year-old granddaughter. I was devastated; yet I saw clearly that I could not spare the luxury of depression. I had to rouse my strength and get into action.

****

In truth, I felt I had not been a good mother—to Bill or to Amy, my daughter. I spent my time pursuing career passions, which was unusual for women at the time. I was teaching, working after school, and running a household—I had none of this thing they now call "quality time" with my own kids. Even when Bill died, I was in the middle of a master's degree in Visually Handicapped Studies. In my thirst for knowledge, there has never been such a thing as disability.

In the midst of our deep mourning, Amy once said to me, "How lucky you are, Mom. You have a second chance to raise a thirteen-year-old girl, which is no small task." And it was true. With Christine, I had a second chance at motherhood. After Bill died I moved into his house so as to disrupt Christine's life as little as possible. The first year was a multilayered experience of coping: coping with Bill's death (by far the greatest loss of my life); coping with putting away the pots and pans so I could find them; coping with learning to read Braille; coping with the labyrinth of social services I had to procure for Christine and myself; coping with teenage music; coping with nurturing my granddaughter while trying to realize my own aspirations; and coping with the homework, both mine and hers. How could I help her with her homework?

As it turned out, the blindness that I imagined as such a handicap was in fact my greatest asset. One day we sat down with her algebra homework. I was paralyzed. "How am I going to help her?" I wondered. She had to read the problems to me, slowly and clearly. Then I realized that there wasn't much for me to do. Because Christine had to read so slowly and carefully, she had time to think, to see, to observe.

Once she had an assignment to write a paper on Keats's "Ode On a Greecian Urn." I thought to myself, "Why in heaven's name do the schools torture these children with this purple prose of thees and thous?" but of course I didn't say this to my granddaughter. So she read, and I listened. And as I listened, blanketed in darkness, the words came to life. Reading aloud gave us both an appreciation of words—their sound, their meaning—that silent reading cannot convey.

And there I discovered that out of the loss of eyesight came the revelation of insight. In-sight.

Life was not ending. A new life was beginning. We explored the joys of learning together, and together we created a new social life, right in our own home. We created a community. Although my actual family was limited to Christine, Amy, and Amy's husband, Bruce, my extended family was made up of the "bouquet of friends" that Bill bequeathed to me, and of Christine's friends—young, needy people whose home lives were perhaps less than ideal. So we celebrated—we had dinner parties three times a week to keep our spirits up and to remind us both that life goes on—at any age.

****

Now Christine is a young woman and lives in the flat below. She has traveled, gotten her second bachelor's degree, and is working with blind people. I am here in Bill's house, at eighty-two, planning my next set of adventures and enjoying the quiet, soothing vibes of the place.

Once, when I was deep in the throes of grief, I asked one of my professional friends what he knew of the afterlife. His answer was unusual. "Listen to the birds," he said. "They know things. They'll tell you." Today I sit on my deck as the birds come and go. I've begun to recognize their songs—the heartbroken twitter of sparrows, the frenzied call of crows—and each of them brings me a piece of Bill's heart, as if he were looking over my shoulder and saying, "You're doing just fine, Mom. You're just fine."

PART 2
PARENTS & CHILDREN

HEARING CASSANDRA

by Susan Palmer

Like Cassandra, I understand the meaning of a siege. Only my world will not fall in fire but in disease. Multiple sclerosis surrounds me like an invading army. No one is left to plead my case. Those who provided hope have long since fallen. No treaty is in sight. Only with time will I know if Mercy will be granted. I find no peace in knowing how my world will end and, like Cassandra, there is no one to listen.

We all live knowing we will die. We pass Cassandra in the halls, not hearing or pretending not to hear. We do not seek shelter elsewhere. There is comfort in the familiar, even as it crumbles. We listen to old scratched records and remember when we bought them, who we were then.

I have a beautiful daughter. I wonder if I will ever see her face. Photographs are taken just in case. I hear Cassandra whisper words, but I refuse to listen. The walls are weakening. The army, growing in strength, awaits. Yet I persist, not understanding why. I do not run. Perhaps because there is nowhere to go. Perhaps because there is no more to understand.

On good days, I spend more time at work than with my husband. I type frantically, listening to Cassandra pace. What if I can't finish my work? What if my brain slows? I need to share so many ideas, so many dreams. I smile at my partner, my companion. I know he is beginning to understand. Soon he will carry the flag, but not today. My disease and my blindness are part of his education, part of my own. I laugh at his jokes and wonder if my speech is slurred. Still, not knowing why, I continue to write and dream. I smile under stress, in sadness and in pain.

On good days, I am annoyed that my husband asks for help to complete the tasks I know he can do alone. Even on the best days, I am tired, always tired. I put the laundry away. I wash the dishes and empty the trash—for as long as I can. I know it will not last.

I want to buy a house. I owned one once, and now with the thought of a new one comes fear. Getting what I want will someday mean losing it. The loss will be so much greater if I care. But how can I not care?

It takes me three good days to face up to each bad day. I am not certain if it is hope or denial that eventually expires. After three days, I see the break in the line and the section of wall that fell to dust. I understand the threat. Yet in the dark stillness, I hear a song that makes me weep. I think it is an old Celtic song, or perhaps the hymn, that makes us human. The sound falls too far away for me to be certain of the words, but I am certain of the tune.

In some ways, my bad days are my best days. There is no fuel for frantic thoughts, only the tired ache of sadness. But mourning comes only with the loss of something dear. I know how much I have to lose. For this I am blessed, not cursed. In the dark times, I hear the sadness in my husband's voice. I know we are both under siege. He chooses to stay.

In the darkness, we can both hear Cassandra's voice. It is louder than before.

In the darkness, we see each other and pretend not to hear. My husband takes my hand and kisses it. In that moment, there is no disease, and time does not pass.

In ancient mythology, Cassandra was the daughter of Priam, King of Troy. She was endowed with the gift of true prophesy but fated by Apollo never to be believed.

JACKSON'S DISEASE

by Chana Jackson

I never imagined I would end up on this path: I am the mother of two boys who are blind. There is no history of visual impairment in my family, or my husband's, and yet here we are.

For the first few hours after our son Nicholas was born, everything seemed fine. We experienced all the typical things new parents do and had the most perfect baby in the world. When the pediatrician came in a few hours later and said, "I think there's a problem with Nicholas's eyes," I thought my heart was going to stop. After countless tests and exams, we knew Nicholas was blind. There was some difficulty in arriving at a diagnosis, but eventually the doctors settled on PHPV (persistent hyperplastic primary vitreous), a condition that is not genetic. It was an overwhelming experience to go through, and thirteen years after the fact I remember it vividly.

Although we'd never known anyone who was blind and were consumed with what it meant for our son, we quickly found that the most important thing about Nicholas was that he was a baby. Being worried about things like his career was a lot less important than figuring out how to get him to sleep through the night! We were lucky enough to be living in an area where there were numerous resources, and when Nicholas was a few weeks old we found the Blind Babies Foundation. Here we found the experts we needed to answer our endless questions.

The Foundation sent a home counselor to visit us on a regular basis, and we learned about stimulating Nicholas's senses with things such as textured quilts and tactile toys.

There was so much to learn, but early on we realized that much of what we were doing was just good parenting and not specific to a visually impaired child. This was the most important lesson we learned over the years: although we may be doing our work in Braille and adapting the world to work for blindness, blindness is just a characteristic and not a definition.

Nicholas grew and developed normally, and we adjusted to life as parents. When Nicholas was three years old, we had another son, Ryan. We were stunned to discover he was also blind. The doctors had been certain the condition was not genetic, and yet it was. This was a difficult shock to absorb, but for different reasons from when Nicholas was born. We were no longer worried that we didn't know what to do with a blind baby—we'd conquered that already—but we were consumed with worry over the genetic problem that was responsible for our sons' blindness. What other symptoms might be lurking about?

We began a long and tedious process, familiar to many parents of children with undiagnosed conditions, of trying to place a name on our genetic anomaly. None of the options matched our histories, and those that were close seemed terrifying, with all kinds of frightening additional problems. In the end, we settled for not being able to put a name on the condition. Our DNA did not quite match the most likely suspect, so we decided it was "Jackson's disease," where the main identifier is incredibly adorable boys. When the boys are older, and particularly if they are thinking about having children of their own, we will probably go back on the diagnosis hunt, but until then we continue to accept the unknown.

Nicholas continued to develop normally and hit the various developmental milestones at the appropriate times. Ryan, however, experienced delays, especially with regard to language. We were not overly concerned at first because he seemed generally to be moving in the right direction, but as time passed the delays became more and more pronounced. He continues to progress, but very much at his own pace. We have two blind children, but they are on very different paths. Nicholas, at thirteen, has been mainstreamed for the past few years and is a bright academic student. Ryan, aged ten, has also been mainstreamed now, but he has communication problems that we are still trying to untangle. Both boys are both wonderful and gifted in many ways.

There have been numerous outstanding teachers and agencies along the way that have helped us find the resources we needed, and we have been fortunate in experiencing a wide range of educational programs. The boys have gone from classes that teach kids with a variety of handicaps to classes with all visually impaired children to being mainstreamed with "typical" kids. Segregated classes and full-inclusion settings have been valuable for both boys at various times. We try to look at their individual needs and remember that these needs change over time. The perfect program last year may be a poor one this year. In all of their programs, though, there has been one constant: the importance of Braille. My husband and I learned Braille when the boys were little and have always tried to provide lots of books and exposure to the written word.

No life is without struggle. We have certainly had difficult times, and I'm sure the future holds more, but with the support of family, friends, and our belief in God, we have always found a way to the other side. With two blind children, our family's problems are easy for others to see, but in fact we are all carrying burdens of some sort.

I would never have wished for my boys to be blind, but I don't think it's the worst thing that could have happened to them. Lacking eyesight is much less of a handicap than lacking compassion, for example. Nicholas and Ryan are living with two parents who love them beyond description and are part of a large, wonderful extended family. They are growing up loved for being who they are, and that's a pretty great thing.

A BAG THAT'S FULL

by Nicholas Jackson

My name is Nicholas Jackson, and I was born totally blind. It was caused by some disease I don't have a name for. But now, thirteen years later, I don't feel there are many barriers to overcome as a result of being blind. In fact, I think being blind isn't much different from having sight. The only difference I see is that blind people have another way of doing things. But eventually blindness becomes a part of everyday life.

Although being blind has its disadvantages, my opinion is that they are very small. Most of the time I don't notice them. I think a visually impaired person can do most things a sighted person can do, but it takes practice. I've done things like identifying red and green lights by the direction traffic is moving. I've learned to cook several dishes, for example an artichoke fritata and an English muffin pizza. But these are only some of the things I can do that a sighted person can do. I've done other things, too.

I've gone rock climbing and participated in a ropes course, which can be scary for some sighted people because they tend to look down from high above the ground. One of the most challenging things I've accomplished is the wall at outdoor school. Each person had to climb the wall while others hold them up. The thing that was so challenging was that no staff were allowed to help.

I've even participated in a sports car rally through the Braille Institute, where I am a student. Each sports car has one student and one driver. The student is the navigator, and he tells the driver where they have to go from a clipboard with the instructions.

As I said before, I don't think being blind is much different from being sighted. It's only a challenge that's been placed into the bag of experiences. My bag of experiences is an imaginary bag that becomes fuller when I undergo challenges beyond my comfort zone. If I stay in my comfort zone and don't undertake any challenges, the bag will be closer to empty. I'd rather have a bag that's full.

MY FATHER

by Kathy Dempsey

I became interested in working with the blind and visually impaired because of my dear father, who became totally blind due to retinitis pigmentosa. He was the best friend and nicest dad—or maybe nicest friend and best dad—I could ever have. I grew up in Pasadena, California, where my dad held a variety of jobs before he started losing more and more of his vision. After his vision was gone altogether he landed a job through the Business Enterprise Program, a federal organization that trains blind and low-vision people to manage and operate small restaurants, cafeterias, and newspaper stands.

We moved to San Bernadino in 1957. My father bought a house there from a blind friend and continued his career as a cafeteria manager. I remember him as a hard worker. He was incredibly good with voices. Someone would come up and say, "Hi, Earl," and he would say, "Hi, Joe, did you catch some trout over the weekend?" He had a fantastic capacity for identifying voices and remembering details about people he met. My father was a well-liked and friendly guy.

Dad operated a cash register where he worked, and this was before the advent of talking calculators and cash registers. Even so, he knew where all the currency and coins were. It was astonishing the way he would add all of the items in his head. Someone would say, "Earl, I've got a cheeseburger, a large Coke, a bag of potato chips, and two Milky Ways," and my dad would calculate it all in his head and say, "That will be three dollars and eighty-five cents." He would have to trust the person to give him the proper denomination of money, of course, and occasionally we would find one-dollar bills where the tens were supposed to be; bills for which my father had given change for a ten.

If dad dropped a coin on the floor, he'd ask me, "Kitty, could you please pick up that dime I dropped?" I'd say, "Dad, how do you know that was a dime?"

"I can tell the difference between the coins by the sound they make when they hit the tile," he'd reply, and sure enough, I'd look, and there would be a dime. Sometimes he'd even let me keep it. He could tell if I was rattling around in the candy. Once in a while he'd tell me that if I asked for some Lifesavers it would probably be okay. I couldn't get away with much when I was growing up, even though my father was blind.

I remember how he would sometimes wish he could still see me. He'd hoped he would still be able to make out my features when I turned sixteen, but after I was thirteen most of his vision was gone. When I became interested in painting and started winning awards and art scholarships, my dad regretted that he couldn't appreciate my work visually. That was hard for me.

Sometimes Dad would become depressed and lethargic. Mom would say, "Let's take a drive up to the mountains," and Dad would say, "Why should I go? I can't see them, anyway." Nevertheless, he had many different interests. One of the biggest was music. Dad had a good voice, and he played the piano by ear. He enjoyed listening to big bands and swing, and he liked dancing, so he and my mom would go to dances. Dad also loved sports. He would listen to all the basketball games, all the Dodger baseball games, and he absolutely loved the Los Angeles Rams. I was an only child, and a girl to boot, but since I was around my dad all the time I became quite a sports fan. In fact, I'm much more of a sports fan than my husband.

My father died in 1982, and I miss him terribly. He was an inspiration to me. Everyone he met liked him, and I have memories of him always being out and about in the community. Sometimes we'd sit down in a restaurant and the waitress would come up and ask me, "What does he want?" Whereupon my dad would say, "Hello, I'm over here. I'll tell you what I want." But he would always do it in a polite way. He would remind people that even though he had a disability, he was still his own person. It was important to him to always try and make eye contact when speaking with someone. He thought that made a difference. I think it did, too. He made good eye contact even though he couldn't see where he was looking.

Once I became interested in working with visually impaired people, I discovered there were only two schools in the entire state of California that offered specialist credentials for visually impaired teachers. One was California State University in Los Angeles, which is where I got my degree. One summer, while still in college, I taught at a school for the blind in Hollywood, and I also worked at Dodger Stadium as a waitress and souvenir-seller for five years. I confess to getting a bit tired of baseball after that.

Some time later, while looking for a new job, I noticed an opening for a teacher in Monterey County. I remembered how beautiful that area was, and I thought working there would be like living and working in paradise. That was the first position I applied for, and after one interview, I was hired on the spot. I've been working there ever since.

When I started out in Monterey County I was an itinerant teacher for the first three years, traveling around from school to school providing blind and visually impaired students with books and instruction. I had a mobile classroom in a van with a desk and chairs and lots of other equipment and materials. I would pull the kids out of class and teach them various lessons, including Braille. It was fun for me, and the novelty of leaving class and going out to the van to work was a novelty many of the students enjoyed. Other kids didn't like it because they felt they were being singled out for being different; it all depended on the individual personalities involved.

I've had so many wonderful students over the years. One, who was blind due to albinism, hated to touch type. It was a chore for her, and it was wonderful when we finally got electric typewriters, but even then she didn't like it much. When she called years later to invite me to her college graduation, she said, "Oh, Kathy, thank you for never giving up on me and for insisting that I learn touch typing." She told me she's a whiz on the computer now. She said she has "flying fingers."

I had a little boy named Dan for a pupil. Dan was a very bright boy who was totally blind yet fearless, curious, and unusually verbal. He had what I would call a "motor mouth." He liked to talk and ask questions. Actually, a lot of blind and visually impaired people are extremely verbal. It's a way of having contact with others. Where you and I have the satisfaction of seeing other people around us and knowing they are there, a blind person doesn't have that luxury, so they'll sometimes talk just for the sake of engaging you.

Dan used to talk about the classroom and how it smelled when he walked in. When he was five he asked me, "Kathy, why do molecules move?" I thought, Oh, boy, we've got a bright one here. Not knowing the answer to his question, I suggested we would have a lesson on using reference books so he would learn how to look up molecules; then we could find the answer to his question together. He was an intrepid little boy. He used to ride his bike with his cane sticking out to touch the trees or the fence as he passed by. Needless to say, he fell off and hurt himself all the time, but he would always pick himself up, dust himself off, and start over again.

Dan would ask his sighted guides to describe the cover art on his favorite albums. Then he would go up to another person and tell them all about it, fooling them into thinking he could see. He was a very musical boy, and I still have all of his music. He was fortunate enough to own a keyboard with a variety of rhythms and sounds built into it, and he would create wonderful lyrics and music using these features. These days he's a musician, and he plays something like eight instruments. He's in college now, and he plays in a band called the Blues Hounds.

There's another little boy named Cody Burns who is very much like Dan in that he's inquisitive and bright and verbal and full of fun. I really believe the ability to have fun, enjoy life, and have a sense of humor about yourself and others is key, especially for anyone with a disability. Cody is blessed with all of those attributes. He's from a family who loves him dearly, and he's very secure. He has a good sense of people, and he's considerate of others. I find that most of my students are considerate and think about other people's feelings, possibly because they have to rely on others to help them. I'd say the majority of my students over the years have been unusually nice, gentle, and considerate people.

One day Cody and I were working on an addition problem, five plus five, and I said, "If you don't have your tactile number lines in front of you, you can always count on your fingers." I told him I still do sometimes myself, and I asked, "Well, how many fingers do you have?" He wasn't sure, and when he counted them, he somehow came up with thirteen. These days we still tease him about having thirteen fingers, and he always takes it well.

I've had lots of silly kids, and some are obviously easier to work with than others, but mostly I can say that I love working with blind and visually impaired students. They are incredibly special to me. They're the reason I love my job.

THE THOM FAMILY STORY

by Jeff Thom

Introduction

The three major characters in this story are me, my wife, Leslie, and our four-year old daughter, Andrea. We can't speak for Andrea, but neither Leslie nor I consider ourselves overly heroic or to have accomplished feats that are particularly worth writing home about. But if our stories can inspire anyone, or at least provide some comic relief, we will be more than satisfied.

Jeff

I am a forty-five-year old blind male. In some ways, I am a true man of the '90s. I enjoy spending lots of time with Andrea, I do not feel threatened by my female colleagues at work, and I cook at least as well and often as does Leslie. On the other hand, I also have certain male chauvinistic pig tendencies. I love watching sports, and one of my favorite pastimes is becoming totally absorbed in a football game.

At times I can be too possessive and domineering, although I usually soften in my attempts to assert my delusional male superiority. But let's start from the beginning.

I was born in Santa Rosa, California, on April 30, 1953. Like many other people born in that era, my blindness was caused by the fact that I was born three months premature. My birth weight was approximately 2.5 pounds. At the time of my birth, my parents were faced with the alternatives of almost certain blindness or probable death for their infant son. I for one am more than content with the outcome.

I spent the first year of my life in Santa Rosa and the next two in San Francisco. When I was three, my parents and my sister, Christine, who is three years my senior, moved to Redwood City, about twenty-five miles south of San Francisco. A sign located at one end of this suburban mecca, which has apparently been there for over fifty years, boasts "Weather Best by Government Test." I must admit I have never lived in a place with better weather than Redwood City. I lived there until I went away to college, and I spent my summers there until I completed law school.

We all know how important the first five years of life are to a person's development, and I could bore you with stories I've been told about those years of my life. As an illustration of the freedom my parents gave me to experience the world around me, it may be worth mentioning one of the few events about which I have even a vague memory. One day in preschool, while climbing a ladder up to a slide, I fell off and cracked my chin open, and a few years later I cracked it open again by falling off my porch at home. I leave the reader to deduce what impact, if any, these traumatic events may have had on me. A blind child will usually not be quite as active as his sighted counterparts during the first few years of life, but my parents gave me every freedom I could have asked for.

I am able to remember some important events in my life, starting around the age of six: my sister and I made our first visit to Disneyland, my tonsils were removed, and I began first grade. From first through fourth grade I was bussed across town so that I could attend the same elementary school as all the other blind children from Redwood City. We spent most of our day in regular classes, but part of our time was devoted to instruction in Braille and other special skills. By the start of second grade I was in the top reading group. Academically, at least, I was on my way to early success. Not until law school did I again become a merely average student.

Nineteen sixty-three was an important year for me. That fall, I started the fifth grade in my own neighborhood elementary school, and I believe I was the first blind student in my school district ever to do so. My fifth grade teacher, Mrs. Beaty, was one of the best teachers I ever had, and she had a profound influence on me.

Thanks largely to my mother's insistence, the school district allowed me to start taking trumpet lessons. This was done over the strenuous objections of the music department supervisor. I was just an average trumpet player, but I enjoyed the music and the camaraderie with my sighted friends. In junior high and high school, playing the trumpet saved me from having a much lonelier existence. I continued playing throughout my undergraduate years in college.

While I'm on the subject, I cannot pass up the opportunity to relate an instance of a person taking credit for something when in fact they deserve absolutely none. When I was in the eighth grade, my mother overheard the music supervisor—the very same one who had tried to prevent me from taking trumpet lessons to begin with—make a comment to someone about what an outstanding musician I was, and that it would never have happened but for his intervention.

In sixth grade I was placed in a class for gifted students. Each student attended this class once a week at a designated school in Redwood City. The class was taught by Mr. Mitchell, another of my favorite teachers. It was one of the most broadening experiences of my life. We studied everything from photography to the stock market, and learned how laws are made and how they are enforced.

I've always enjoyed heated political discussions. From the time I was very young, my father encouraged me to debate political issues with him. One time I demonstrated my argumentativeness in school by disputing a statement made by my state senator during a class visit to Sacramento—much to the embarrassment of my mother, who was chaperoning the trip. The senator was later convicted of a minor felony, allowing me to gleefully (and erroneously) conclude that righteousness was on my side in whatever issue we happened to be debating.

During elementary school, however, I began to develop a tendency that would have far-reaching affects on my life. I did not dislike other blind people, but I found I did not particularly want to be like them. Blind people played the piano and the autoharp, so I played the trumpet. Blind people attended summer camps for the blind; therefore, I had absolutely no desire to attend. My attention was focused on the sighted world around me. I think I probably concentrated more on academic and nonsocial pursuits because of this attitude, and it is quite possible I would not be as successful professionally today if my attitude had been different.

On the other hand, my reluctance to become involved with other blind children has had several negative consequences. For one thing, it is very difficult for a blind child to avoid feeling inferior when competing against sighted counterparts. Take the example of playing games. In games that require vision, you simply can't play as well as sighted kids, and it is unlikely that you will even be asked to participate very often. This leads to feelings of isolation that only exacerbate one's inferiority complex.

Even if your parents are reasonably permissive in letting you roam the neighborhood, as mine were, a blind child is not necessarily on a level social playing field with sighted children. When you come from a small family, as I did, and you lack siblings to help propel you into the neighborhood flow, it is even worse. On the other hand, when you participate in activities with other blind people, you do so as an equal. I believe successful social interaction with one's blind peers is of the utmost importance in building self-esteem during childhood.

For this reason, many blind people argue that blind children should be educated primarily in special schools for the blind. I don't deny that under certain circumstances this may be advisable, but I do not feel the social problems created by mainstreaming a blind child are sufficient reason to forego the benefits derived from early exposure to the sighted world. Rather, I think it is essential that a blind child be provided with a multitude of opportunities to participate in activities with his blind peers. I believe just as much harm can occur by separating a blind child from blind peers as can occur by sheltering him from the sighted world, which he will eventually have to live in.

Junior high school and high school were productive but lonely times for me. I did extremely well academically, and I was involved with school band, orchestra, and other extracurricular activities such as student government and the wrestling team. I even had a few good friends. However, I was in many ways an outsider. This stood in contrast to my intelligent sister, who never studied (and who consequently received very poor grades) but who was always at the center of social activity. That didn't do much for my self-esteem. I suspect, however, that by getting all the attention from our parents, and receiving constant accolades for my various accomplishments, I didn't exactly make her feel great about herself, either. It is a real wonder—and a great credit to my sister—that we now have a very loving relationship. This may be partly because she lives in Illinois and has to put up with my presence only occasionally.

During high school, I had my first epileptic seizure. Although I have had no major seizures since my early twenties and the epilepsy has had little impact on my daily life, I still have minor problems when I don't eat or sleep enough or when I fall into bad habits with my medication. Nevertheless, epilepsy is a scary thing to deal with, even for people like me who are not subject to major seizures. I cannot imagine what it must be like to lose consciousness or have the problems that people suffering from severe epilepsy must endure.

As time wore on, the most difficult things for me to handle were not being invited to social functions, and my absolute failure with sighted girls. Unfortunately, I will never know to what degree I might have succeeded because not until college—and even then only rarely—did I even ask them out. I was utterly convinced of my inferiority. I firmly believe that if I had participated in more activities with other blind people my self-esteem would have been raised to a point where my social inhibitions diminished. If I were now single I would be much less inhibited about asking out any woman I was attracted to.

As a result of my inexperience with women—and against the advice of many people—I entered into a disastrous marriage a year after completing law school. I stuck with the marriage for seven years for the sake of our two children, but in retrospect it never really had any chance of succeeding. The specifics are far too personal for me to air here, but a brief recounting might serve to illustrate the consequences of mistakes that were made long ago. The responsibility for these mistakes rests in part with my parents, but primarily I blame myself. It is my hope that these thoughts will be of benefit to other blind people and their families.

I would like to stress that any mistakes my parents made were more than offset by the good choices they made. Both of them fought hard to ensure that I would have the best education possible. My father, although he was away at least a week every month, spent countless hours playing catch with me, watching sports with me, and doing other things that contributed to a positive sense of myself as a male. Blind males—often due to the lack of an attentive father, other times because they don't engage in the physical activities common to most sighted boys—fail to develop an adequate sense of self. I am grateful to my father for his attitudes toward me. Most of all, I am proud of my parents because they rarely tried to prevent me from attempting whatever it was I wanted to do.

In 1971, I began my college career at Willamette University in Salem, Oregon. Here, in addition to political science and economics, I learned a lot about rain. (Too much rain can be depressing, but I still prefer the rain in Oregon to the stifling summer heat in Sacramento, my current home.) Aside from some lonely weekends, I greatly enjoyed my years at this small liberal arts institution. I was well-liked on the whole, but even so I had few close friends. This is an unfortunate trend that I am even now struggling to overcome.

Over the years, very few people have taken a strong dislike to me, but equally few have become my close friends. It may be my diminished self-esteem that lies at the root of this problem. I would encourage any qualified blind person who can afford it to attend school away from home. Going away to college enables a person to experience so many new things and to spread their wings. It also forces you to start making mature choices.

August 1, 1975, was a somewhat memorable day for me. After being rejected by a number of lower echelon law schools—perhaps with good reason—and not knowing what in the world I would do with my future, I was overjoyed to receive notification from Stanford University that they had accepted my application to law school. The Stanford campus was only about thirty miles south of my parents' home, so I was able to visit them on weekends and enjoy some great home cooking. I was only a C student in law school, but I competed with the best and the brightest from around the country. I feel my degree from Stanford helped to ensure my future employment at a time when it was even more difficult for blind lawyers to find work than it is now.

I worked extraordinarily hard throughout most of law school, and even harder while preparing for the California bar exam. I was rewarded with admission to the bar in 1978. Computer technology has helped the blind in school and in the workplace, but even so we still rely on cassette tapes and individuals to read books to us. There is no doubt that a blind person must work harder than his sighted equal to accomplish the same amount in college. However, just as with sighted students, the twin pillars of ability and ambition serve to separate the high achievers from the rest of the pack.

Although I had sporadic contact with blind friends from the Redwood City area, I knew little about issues of concern to the blind community. Nor did I seek out the company of other blind people. In law school, though, I began to realize that not only did I have a stake in the concerns that all blind people share, but I also began to feel an unexpected sense of kinship with other blind individuals. This is not to say that blindness is the only way, or even the primary way, that I bond with others. I also enjoy being with other attorneys, football fans, and anyone who dislikes Rush Limbaugh.

In September of 1978, while awaiting my bar exam results, I moved to Los Angeles to work as a disabled rights attorney. The work was enjoyable, but I did not feel I possessed the characteristics that are necessary to be a great courtroom lawyer. I continued to be involved with the blind community, and as my contacts with blind people increased, I began to come out of my shell. It was during this time that I met my wife. People who met me only after my graduation from law school are startled when I tell them I used to be an extremely shy person.

A year after meeting one another, Leslie and I were married, and within a week of our wedding, we moved to Sacramento, where I began working with the California Legislative Counsel Bureau. I am still employed there after nineteen years. This nonpartisan state agency serves as the attorney for all 120 members of the state legislature. Our primary task is to draft bills and write legal opinions for every member of the legislature. I have experience in many areas of law, but my main expertise lies in the areas of health and human services.

Working for the Legislature is not your typical 8-to-5 job. At times I put in very long hours, including nights and weekends. I must continually meet multiple short deadlines, and thus the work can be very stressful. On the other hand, there are certain times of the year, such as autumn, when I can take time off because the Legislature is not in session and the workload is greatly reduced. I have worked in a number of controversial areas, such as MediCal reform (California's Medicaid program) and welfare reform.

I confess to taking great pride in my work. I feel that I work well with legislative staff, lobbyists, and legislators. I try to go the extra mile in order to ensure that my work accurately reflects the intent of the individual I am representing. Over the years, I have developed a reputation as a trusted, knowledgeable, and hardworking attorney. I work with a talking computer, using Braille when the situation calls for it, and I have an assistant who reads documents to me when necessary.

I believe my greatest failing is not that I occasionally make mistakes (which I do), but that I try too hard and put too much emphasis on my job performance. I think it is more important to evaluate one's own performance—if this can be done objectively—than to worry inordinately about the views of one's superiors. I am aware that there is always room for improvement. Speaking frankly, though, I think I have performed at a level that should have led to greater advancement than I have received, and this view is echoed by many of my sighted peers. But the older I get, the more I realize that my family life is more important than my vocation. I often wish I had come to this realization years ago.

In 1981 my son, Paul, was born in Carmichael, California, near Sacramento; and in 1983 my daughter Michelle was born at the same hospital. I could write a tome about my experiences with Paul and Michelle, but this is not the time or place. Perhaps my biggest failure as a parent (and something I am trying to change with my youngest child, Andrea) is that I spent too much time imposing the discipline my ex-wife refused to provide.

In retrospect, I think I should have concentrated on providing more love and understanding. But I would summarize what I have learned with the observation that blind parents in this country, although they have some unique difficulties with which to deal, must generally cope with the same problems as their sighted counterparts. Our blindness has remarkably little to do with our ability to succeed or fail in these endeavors.

Leslie is already starting to creep into this narrative. Rather than begin a discussion of the period in which our lives have been intertwined, I will turn over the reins of this story to her. I leave you with the promise (or the threat, however you choose to take it) that I will return to haunt these pages later on.

Leslie

I was born the sixth of seven children in Montebello, California, on February 27, 1963. My mother was a stay-at-home mom, while my father drove a truck for a large supermarket chain.

When I was about a year-and-a-half old, my mother noticed that something was wrong with one of my eyes. She could actually see into the eye, and it looked like what she called a "cat's eye." I also had two cysts on my left eye, and during their removal my eyes were examined to determine what was wrong. It was discovered that I had retinoblastoma, a form of eye cancer that occurs in early childhood and is usually inherited. I was referred to UCLA Medical Center for treatment, and the concensus was that my right eye had to be removed. During the procedure, tumors were discovered on my left eye that required treatment with chemotherapy.

At the time the use of chemotherapy drugs was still extremely experimental, and one of the drugs I was given induced a stroke. The stroke caused temporary paralysis on the left side of my body, and I had to relearn how to walk. I have never fully regained the coordination and strength in my left arm and leg, and I have a very limited ability to manipulate objects with my left hand.

It was very difficult for my parents to understand and cope with what was going on. Even the best facilities—and UCLA Medical Center was one—did not have social workers and other personnel to help families in coping with these types of problems. They did try to work with me as best they could, though. Since UCLA Med Center was located a long way from my parents' home, I spent a lot of time in the hospital by myself. My father's work schedule limited the time he had to visit me, and my mother often had to be home with my siblings.

With the more limited understanding of cancer that existed in 1964, it wasn't known what my odds were of living through this ordeal. For four years I was in and out of UCLA Medical Center. Sometimes things went well and the doctors would say everything looked fine. Other times tumors would appear and hope would start to wane. In addition to chemotherapy, I had to undergo cobalt treatments and laser therapy. Although my mother did not fully understand what was going on, she kept a notebook during that time, and her notes have given me a limited amount of information and insight into those early years of my life. Years later, when our daughter Andrea started having her own retinoblastoma treatments, I reread this journal in order to compare her course of treatment with what I had to undergo.

By the time I was five, it was determined that all the sight would eventually be lost in my left eye, so the doctors decided to remove the eye altogether. Foundations such as Make A Wish did not yet exist, but the hospital staff got together and raised enough money for my whole family to go to Disneyland before my eye was removed. With limited depth perception in that eye, I remember being afraid of even walking across the pedestrian bridges at Disneyland. If I stopped to look at something and my family got ahead of me, I became paralyzed with fear.

Just a week before my eye was to be removed, I was told that the vision in my left eye was almost normal. However, a tumor can get out of control so rapidly as to completely change the situation, which is what happened in my case. At the time my left eye was removed in May 1968, my parents were told I probably had very little time to live. This was the case with most people born with retinoblastoma at the time.

In light of my now-total blindness and the newly optimistic projections about my life expectancy, my parents enrolled me in a special elementary school for the blind in Los Angeles. I went there from kindergarten through sixth grade. We were bussed to school from all different parts of Los Angeles county, and I had the longest bus ride of all.

In many ways, it was a great experience. I was able to meet and become lifelong friends with many visually impaired children. We not only spent all our time together at school, but also on those long bus rides. We were taught not only the things all school children learn, but also special skills such as Braille or reading large print. I think it is much better if both Braille and academic subjects are taught by a single teacher. In my case, Braille was taught once or twice a week by one teacher and academic subjects were taught daily by another teacher. This is also how most mainstreamed blind children are taught in regular school settings, but unlike regular school teachers, ours could help us with Braille material.

I left home between 5:30 and 6:00 in the morning for a school day that began at 9:00, and didn't return home until 5:30 or 6:00 in the evening. This cut into the time I had to spend with neighborhood children, but because I had so many brothers and sisters I was treated like one of the gang. I was also able to do a lot of things on nights and weekends with kids from the neighborhood. I owe a profound debt to my family for not trying to shelter me or restrict my activities.

I also liked the idea of not having to compete with sighted peers at school, and I never had to undergo the teasing that frequently occurs when blind kids are mainstreamed into regular schools. I think blind children attending regular schools often develop inhibitions about being different from their sighted classmates, and I was happy that I didn't have to worry about this problem. I became involved in writing stories and plays, and two of them were actually performed by my classmates. We also developed a student newspaper, of which I was the editor, in which we conducted interviews and reported on school activities.

Because my entire left side was severely weakened, I began taking piano lessons during first grade, primarily as a means of building up strength in my left hand. I doubt that a regular school would have afforded me the opportunity to do this. Although I never became a super piano player, I did improve my strength and range of motion in my fingers.

After finishing sixth grade, it was determined that I should attend a regular school for junior high. The program we chose was outside the Los Angeles Unified School District, where we lived, but the bus ride was only about twenty minutes. Had I been placed in a program within my district, I would have had to endure another three-hour bus ride to get to school every day. Thus, I attended South Whittier Intermediate for seventh and eighth grade.

Due to the confidence and academic skills I had acquired in elementary school, I had little difficulty with the junior high school curriculum. There were two partially sighted children attending my school, and we had a resource room we could use for test-taking or writing Braille. The room also served as a depository for Braille materials, such as encyclopedias. Most of the time, though, we attended class with everyone else.

While at South Whittier, I became involved in a number of extracurricular activities, including Spanish Club and a fine arts club composed of forty kids (the twenty most outstanding academic achievers from both grades). Once the club took a week-long trip to Yosemite as a reward for our scholastic achievements. I was actively involved with choir, and I entered spelling bees and writing competitions; in eighth grade I won school competitions in both.

I stayed in the Whittier School District for my first year of high school. Like junior high, this school had a resource room for our special needs, and Braille transcribers were available to put certain materials into Braille for me. However, the farther you go in school, the more materials you need, and for non-sighted students like me, the harder they are to come by.

While I was in eighth grade, something called the Master Plan was put into place. The Master Plan resolved to start sending more and more children to their home schools, and in tenth grade I began attending my local high school, Montebello High. During ninth grade, a low vision student with whom I had been friends since early childhood became a part of my family, and she remained with us through the rest of high school. We were the first two visually impaired students to attend Montebello High School in many years.

Many teachers didn't know what to do with us—whether to give us grades, whether we should participate in class or just observe, etc. Gradually, we educated the teachers as to our capabilities, although the principal refused to let us take swimming because he thought we would drown. The fact that I had been swimming since I was four years old apparently wasn't enough to change his mind. In general, though, I had a great time in high school, and I thrived academically and socially. My academic success got my name placed in two books devoted to America's top high school students.

Extracurricular school activities included choir and performing arts clubs, which performed at Disneyland, among other locales in southern California. I also tutored elementary school students in math and reading. I had an active social life and I attended as many dances as I could, even my Senior Prom. From elementary school through the end of high school I participated in events sponsored by the Foundation for the Junior Blind and the Braille Institute. These included dances, trips to television and motion picture studios, summer and winter camps, and trips to other parts of the country.

I was active in a Catholic youth group, and I sang in the church choir, which not only went on tour but also made a record. I did readings in my own church and around southern California, and wherever we went I made new friends and gained social skills not all blind people are able to acquire. In sum, my school days were a wonderful experience.

During high school I got summer jobs through the Foundation of the Junior Blind, and I had the opportunity to work in a variety of different settings, from a Naval Air Station to a mushroom farm. After graduating from high school, I attended a residential program at the Foundation for the Junior Blind in order to learn independent living skills like cooking and cleaning, and to brush up on other skills like typing, which I would need when I went away to college. Since many of the participants were newly blind and thus had problems dealing with their disability, I became one of the student leaders.

In January 1982, after finishing this program, I enrolled in a junior college in Whittier. I spent two semesters there and did well. A year later I moved to Torrance, about thirty miles from my parents' home, where I lived with friends and obtained my A.A. degree in 1984. I subsequently applied and was accepted to San Francisco State University, where I majored in psychology. My intention was eventually to earn a graduate degree in special education and go on to teach blind and visually impaired children.

My mother didn't like the idea of my moving far away to a place where I knew hardly a soul, but I adjusted well to life in San Francisco and made many very close and continuing friendships. On the side, I worked for the Special Education Department, correcting papers for students who were learning how to read and write Braille. I also taught blind people how to use a reading machine that provides access to printed material, and I transcribed materials into Braille that were used as a testing instrument for gaining a California teaching credential. Outside of school I remained active in church and with the California Council of the Blind. I also became involved with public transit issues in the Bay Area.

Shortly after moving to San Francisco I began experiencing a problem for which I was totally unprepared: severe migraine headaches. It is a problem I still have today. They may have been caused by my retinoblastoma treatment, although I will probably never know for sure. I was given medication for the headaches, but the only results seemed to be blackouts and increasing depression. I began to lose all desire to attend classes, and I lost all confidence in myself. I took the medication from 1984 until 1986. My blackouts ended when I stopped taking the medication, but I continue to battle depression.

After moving to Sacramento in 1987, I continued taking classes at California State University at Sacramento. I received my bachelors degree in psychology from San Francisco State in 1988. However, the self-confidence I enjoyed prior to moving to San Francisco, and much of my ambition, has never fully returned.

Our Life Together

Note: Although Jeff will serve as the narrator for the rest of this story, the observations contained below belong to both of us.

We first met at a convention of the California Council of the Blind in 1982, an organization in which we are both still active and for whom Jeff currently serves as second vice president. We saw each other at these conventions twice a year for the next three or four years, and we shared several substantial discussions about our lives, including issues involving Jeff's family, Leslie's dislike of school, and her uncertainty about what she wanted to do with her life. After I filed for divorce in 1986 we began dating, and we soon realized that we were very much in love. Marriage is never an easy thing, and as our story will indicate, ours has not always been a bowl of cherries. But I can say unequivocally that I have always felt being with Leslie is the most wonderful thing that has ever happened to me.

Although we agreed to be married in early 1987, I hemmed and hawed about setting a date. Finally, she and her mother told me the date was set, the church reserved, and had I better be there. We were married in Montebello, California, by her brother Kevin, a Catholic priest, on January 7, 1989. You might think that with this being Leslie's first marriage, and with the vast majority of the 400 people in attendance being her friends and relatives, that she would be the nervous one. But she was cool as a cucumber and loved the whole ceremony while I was a nervous wreck.

The Caribbean cruise that followed proved to be an absolutely marvelous honeymoon. We were a bit apprehensive about how we would get around a huge cruise ship, but Leslie went over the layout months ahead of time by reading descriptions supplied by our travel agent, and this helped immensely. We made friends on the cruise, who helped us get around when we went ashore, and we have since gone on several tours with these friends.

Leslie and I have suffered through our share of crises during the course of our marriage. In 1987 Leslie was hit by a van, broke her ankle, and spent several months unable to walk. Then, in 1989, she experienced a disintegrated eardrum, which left her utterly without hearing in her right ear and severely curtailed her capacity to travel independently. Ear surgery was ultimately required, including the grafting of a new eardrum. Leslie believes this episode served to further erode her self-confidence.

These events did, however, help provide the impetus for Leslie to get her first guide dog in 1990. This proved to be a huge success, and now she can scarcely imagine being without a dog. I, on the other hand, will probably always remain a cane user. Any blind person who looks objectively at both methods of travel can see that guide dogs have definite advantages, but they are not for everyone. Moreover, the use of either a dog or a cane does not guarantee that a person will be a good, independent traveler.

In 1988, Leslie started working as office manager for a private nonprofit organization providing services to the blind and visually impaired in the Sacramento area. Not only did she perform well on this job, but she thoroughly enjoyed the work. She especially liked the idea that she was engaging in work that had a real value to the community. Unfortunately, she had to leave this position in 1995. Since then, she has not been able to find anything to fill this void, although she has worked periodically as a saleswoman for a company that sells products for the blind.

Both of us, as I've mentioned, work with the California Council of the Blind. I am involved in several areas, including the setting of policy to better the lives of the blind and visualy impaired. Leslie is currently president of an affiliate organization involved in providing Braille and talking books for library users.

In November 1989, we bought our home, a nice four-bedroom house in the southwestern part of Sacramento. Many sighted friends tell us we are lucky because we don't have to shoulder the cost of a car. On the other hand, we can't do many of the easy home repairs that so many sighted people are able to, and this necessitates extra expenditures on home maintenance. Part of the problem is related to blindness, and part to my total lack of mechanical inclination.

Leslie is far more mechanically inclined than I. Even house cleaning is a problem for me. It is not hard to do basic vacuuming, floor washing, etc., but in order to really make things look spotless a blind person has to be extremely good (or lucky) and an inordinate amount of time has to be expended on these chores. Life in the '90s doesn't seem to give anybody enough time to accomplish these tasks, so we sometimes hire someone to clean the house, thus incurring additional expenses.

Blindness creates other obstacles as well. With the enormous volume of mail any household gets these days, it is necessary for us to have a reader to help us with things like bills and correspondence. We use volunteers when we can, but we often need to hire readers. We also have to secure transportation in order to complete the tasks of daily living. Sometimes we use van services, but these need to be reserved two days in advance. This means when you aren't able to plan ahead for the trip, you have to rely on friends and neighbors for assistance. It is an uncomfortable feeling to be dependent on others. To partly reduce this feeling, we usually pay for whatever assistance we get in ferrying us around, and we also try to do favors for those people who regularly help us.

As with most marriages, there are things that pull us toward one another and things that pull us apart. We both like many of the same things, including concerts, sporting events, and traveling. We both love to read, and I enjoy reading aloud to Leslie. We used to ski, hike, and do other outdoor activities together, but Leslie's physical condition has limited the amount she can do.

Blindness also makes it much harder for Leslie to find a job and establish the type of identity she wants (the unemployment rate for blind Americans is approximately 70%). Blindness inhibits me in seeking social contacts and making close friends. These, along with many other factors, complicate our lives and add stress to our marriage. But we hang in there. We persevere. Even though blindness causes certain specific problems, the basic dynamics of nurturing a marriage are no different for a blind spouse than for a sighted one.

Andrea

Leslie and I strongly desired a child of our own, but the fear that the child would inherit retinoblastoma weighed heavily upon us. Genetic counselling only confirmed our worst suspicions—that the odds were our offspring would have retinoblastoma. But with the recent improvements in treating this disease, we concluded that we should not be deterred from having a child.

The pregnancy was certainly eventful. Early in the first trimester, Leslie became so sick she could not even keep down clear liquids. Her condition ultimately required two hospitalizations and the use of a feeding tube. Leslie's labor was long and painful, but for me, having never been in a delivery room before, participating in the birth process was a wonderful experience. We were overjoyed at the birth of our beautiful daughter, Andrea Lynne Thom, on January 30, 1994; Super Bowl Sunday.

By the time Andrea was three months old, Leslie's confidence in her parenting skills began to increase and life started to assume a degree of normalcy. This was abruptly shattered near the end of April by the not unexpected, but nonetheless depressing, diagnosis that Andi did indeed have retinoblastoma. Within a few days of the diagnosis, Andi began receiving five weeks of radiation therapy in San Francisco. This involved staying in San Francisco on weekdays, and since both of us were working we split the time with Andi. After Leslie's job ended in 1995, though, she has been the one going with Andi most of the time.

In addition to several dozen examinations under anesthesia, Andi has had to undergo laser therapy and cryotherapy (a method of freezing tumors) in order to keep her cancerous tumors in check. For approximately nine months, Andi received chemotherapy every two or three weeks, necessitating three-day visits and hospital stays. She also endured emergency room visits and lengthy hospital stays at the U.C. Davis Medical Center in Sacramento. Without getting into the complexities of the situation, suffice it to say that whenever she had a fever of 101 or higher, she needed to be hospitalized. One such stay at the U.C. Davis Medical Center was for a period of two weeks, requiring both me and my wife to rotate between home and the hospital.

The tumors in Andi's left eye were held in check by the chemotherapy, but chemo's side effects necessitated its cessation in July of 1996. (The side effects included some reversible neurological damage, but in Leslie's case the same side effects could not be held in check and they led to continuing medical problems.) Two months later Andi's left eye hemorrhaged, causing a complete loss of sight in that eye. Since there was no sight left to save, and retaining the eye could mean risking the spread of tumors, it seemed there was little choice but to have her eye removed.

Since then things have improved. Andi's right eye developed small tumors during the last couple of years, but she had not required laser treatments for over a year. She still has to have examinations under anesthesia every month or so, but since the disease usually disappears past the age of six, the prognosis for her right eye is good. Moreover, the vision appears to be very close to normal.

Her retinoblastoma care has been provided by the U.C. San Francisco Medical Center. Dr. Joan O'Brien, her retinoblastoma specialist, and her other doctors and caregivers at U.C.S.F. have been wonderful. I seriously doubt she could have received better care anywhere in the world.

Nonetheless, there is little doubt that Andi's medical condition has had a profound impact on all of us. Not only has her condition created feelings of guilt on my and Leslie's part, but it has placed another burden on us as well: it creates yet another obstacle to Leslie's desire to have a career and develop her own identity. Andi's stepsister, Michelle, frequently helped, both in the hospital and at home, and she developed a close bond with Andi. At times, though, it seems like bad luck just brings on more bad luck. In December 1996, as the result of an ear infection, Andi developed an infected knee, which required emergency surgery to avoid permanent damage. This beautiful little girl has endured so much, even as she continues to bring us such happiness.

In most ways, Andi has been a normal baby, but she has been subject to frequent ear infections, which necessitated the insertion of ear tubes. These ear infections probably accounted for some delay in her verbal development. Now, however, she is—to put it mildly—an extremely verbal child, and her test scores in many areas far exceed those in her age group.

Like so many of the children with cancer we have met over the past four years, Andi is extremely resilient. She is a very outgoing child; not only does she make friends easily, but she wants to be the leader in many situations. When things don't go her way or she can't solve a problem, though, she becomes easily frustrated and angry. She is a curious child, and according to many who know her, quite intelligent. If this is so, it might be explained by the theory—espoused by many physicians—that people with inherited retinoblastoma often exhibit above-normal intelligence.

Andi is now in her second year of preschool, and she enjoys it mightily. Our one complaint is that she is not provided with enough reading instruction, although better efforts are being made toward achieving this goal during the current school year. Andi loves being read to, and we read books that have both print and Braille to her at least four or five nights a week. We are frustrated, however, by the fact that our blindness limits our ability to teach her reading at an early age. A few months ago we enrolled her in a martial arts class, which she is also thoroughly enjoying. The teacher is not trying to make experts out of these kids, but the class does instill discipline, coordination, and other positive elements in the participants.

Leslie and I have complementary talents in helping Andi learn. Leslie is better at working with Andi's teachers to make sure she gets all the assistance she needs. She is also a more consistent disciplinarian. As for myself, I have always been more willing to play outside with Andi, follow her on her bike, go to the park with her, and do other things that some blind parents find daunting. Sometimes I worry about losing verbal contact with her; Leslie and I know how important it is that Andi grow up with the same wide variety of experiences that a child with sighted parents has.

There are times when my long work hours prevent me from giving Andi as much time as I would like. There are also times when Leslie's legitimate need to have a life of her own outside the family cuts into the amount of time she and Andi are able spend together. Both Leslie and I do what we can to ensure that one or both of us is giving Andi the love and attention she needs. This is a balancing act and is not always easy.

A few words about the Make A Wish Foundation. They have helped many children whose acquaintance we have made during Andi's ordeal. They have certainly helped Andi. We debated long and hard about what Andi's wish should be, so as to get something that would truly be for her, not for us. In the end they gave her a wonderful playground set, for which we shall be forever grateful. We will always remain strong and enthusiastic supporters of this wonderful charity.

But let us return to the impact of Andi's retinoblastoma. From a medical standpoint, it has had several effects. First, she developed an extraordinary high level of spinal pressure during chemotherapy, which led to severe headaches. Although the spinal pressure is now in check and the headaches are no longer as severe or as frequent, she still has migraines and takes medication for this problem. There is still a chance that new tumors may develop in her right eye over the next couple of years, something we worry about all the more due to Leslie's late onset of tumors in her left eye. Unfortunately, Andi's risk of having some other form of cancer during her lifetime appears to be greater than average and, unless medical science makes some kind of breakthrough in the next fifteen or twenty years, there is also a good chance her own children could inherit retinoblastoma.

There are also some nonmedical consequences resulting from this disease. We feel sure that she would naturally have been a strong-willed child. But the frequent shots and blood tests, her experiences with anesthesia, the insertion of intravenous tubes, and the use of feeding tubes during chemotherapy have created in Andi a hatred of confinement. For no apparent reason she will get hysterical about being restrained in an infant seat, or if we restrain her to prevent her from being hurt. She screams that she is being hurt when she isn't even being touched if she thinks it will help her get her way. These hysterical tantrums used to last up to an hour. She still has occasional lengthy tantrums, but they have diminished markedly of late. We hope and believe that Andi's problems have strengthened her and made her more capable of dealing with whatever challenges lie ahead in her life.

All three of us have overcome many barriers, and we know that many challenges are still ahead. It would be silly to deny that blindness is not responsible for some of these barriers. However, blind people who use blindness as an excuse for not realizing their goals are no less guilty of perpetuating negative stereotypes about the blind than the sighted people who discriminate against us. So, there is no end to this story. Leslie, Andrea, and I are "a work in progress."

THE STORY OF MY LIFE

by Kimberly Jane Fowell

I was born on January 4, 1967, at Queen of the Valley hospital in Napa, California. I was born visually and hearing impaired, and I became congenitally damaged when I was still an infant. I had to have both my eyes and ears operated on when I was two years old.

When I was living in Napa with my mom and dad, I entered a private pre-school program for very young children with special disabilities. School was very difficult and frightening for me. Due to my learning disability, I was a slow reader, and it was real hard for me not to be able to see or hear very well. People would always make fun of me and tease me about my vision impairment. I was called cross-eyed a whole bunch of times when I was a little girl.

I can read large print or large-typed news letters, although I can read some small print when I am wearing my special reading glasses. Whenever I receive a letter from my mother, she always types it up in large print so it will be easy for me to read. I have been thinking that sometimes I wish I was not visually or hearing impaired, but I have it now. I still do enjoy life, even though I cannot see that well.

When I was two years old I had my ears and my eyes operated on. It was very scary. In August of 1969 I started going to a pre-school program in Napa. It was a special day care program for children who have very special disabilities. I had several eye operations and ear operations when I was four years old. My parents were very worried and frightened when the doctors told them I had vision and hearing problems. Having these things and congenital impairment also was very frightening and sad for me because I was always afraid I would be made fun of.

I wear my special reading glasses when I get a letter in the mail, or when I am doing my budgeting or reading a very important letter from my case manager. My reading glasses are very helpful when I need to read something that is typed in small print. I have lots of Readers Digest large-print books of my own. I do wear a plastic shell over my left eye. I have no sight in my left eye at all. I have been wearing a plastic shell over my left eye for a real long time. If I wasn't wearing a plastic shell I would have to have eye surgery to remove my left eye.

What really makes me angry about my vision impairment is when I try to explain to people why I cannot see very well. I feel like even when I try hard to be patient with my friends, I have to keep explaining myself over and over again. My vision impairment is not something to be afraid of, and my hearing impairment is also something nobody should ever be afraid of.

I am wondering now what will happen if I became totally blind and deaf. It will be really scary for me. I am thinking that when I do become totally blind I will still live in my own apartment and I will still be able to have friends to talk to and to be with. I will always do my own cooking and my own budgeting and manage my own money. What is great is that I am able to do things on my own, such as take the Handy Van to my volunteer job every Monday, Wednesday, and Friday.

My vision impairment does not keep me from learning about life, but it does affect how fast I can read or write. The main problem with being visually and hearing impaired is that when I have to read at my meetings I sometimes get laughed at. I do get help from one of my friends, though. The group I belong to is called People First. It is for people like me who have developmental disabilities.

I have been having all kinds of dreams about what I will do the next time when I go to see my eye doctor, how I will feel if he tells me I have to have eye surgery. If I do have to have surgery, I know that something may go wrong and I could be totally blind for the rest of my life. I will probably be scared and frightened and angry if I lose my sight in my right eye as well as in my left eye. I will still have to cope with my blindness. I would have to use a white cane at all times and wear dark sunglasses.

If I do ever become totally blind at my early age, I would have to order a whole bunch of Braille books from the Lighthouse for the Blind, and I will have to start listening to tapes or talking books from cassettes. I will have to have my own tape recorder. I would have to use a Brailler to type letters in Braille. A long time ago my mother and I talked about how I should handle myself when I go out to see my friends, what I will do if I get made fun of because I cannot see very well or hear very well.

I did think about the time when I had both of my eyes and my ears operated on. I was scared that I might become totally blind and I would not be able to see at all for the rest of my life. If that had happened, I would have gone to the California School for the Blind. How would my mom and dad feel if I ever became totally blind for good and not be able to see ever again? It will be really hard on my mom, and it will be hard on me. I am still afraid that people and kids will keep on making fun of me forever.

Many years ago, when I was still living in Davis, I would ride my three-wheeled bike to the park. I would also ride it to school. I sometimes hated riding my bike to school because kids would make fun of my three-wheeled bike. They called me a cross-eyed monster.

I remember a long time ago when I was going to Enchanted Hills Camp. I was in the camper and counselor talent show even with my vision impairment. Enchanted Hills Camp and Camp Bloomfield were my favorite camps. I really enjoyed them both very much. I still think about what it would be like if I was totally blind. I would still be able to ride the van on my own, and I will still be able to use the telephone to call my friends, and my mom and dad.

I work in a nursing home in Woodland. I work with real old patients who have bad eyesight like I do. I know what it is like for them. I have a very special friend who is also blind. She cannot see at all. Sometimes I feel angry and upset and frustrated with my vision impairments and my hearing impairments. I am able to do my latch hook rugs, and I am able to use public transportation to go different places I need to go. It is hard sometimes, but I still do it. I live on my own, and I try really hard to get along in life with my disabilities.

The frustrating part about being visually impaired is when I try really hard to do something, such as when I go to my People First conference and make speeches, or when I introduce somebody. When I am doing a talk, I get confused about when to stand up and when to sit down. When I am finished reading my sketches and my speeches, the problem is that because I am visually impaired and hearing impaired, everyone starts yelling and talking to me at the same time. It is real hard for me to know what I am trying to do.

I can still remember going to my outings with Best Buddies, a program sponsored by U.C. Davis for people who have developmental disabilities. I had to drop out of Best Buddies because it was too crazy and confusing. I felt that nobody cared about my problems at all because I had to keep explaining myself over and over again. I feel like sometimes, when I tried to explain what visual and hearing impairment means to me, people make unkind remarks and say that my disabilities are fake. I did not like the way I was treated by my co-workers when I used to work at a sheltered workshop. I was attacked by a girl there. She punched me right in the eye one day and almost popped the plastic shell out of my bad eye.

I have been trying to think happy and positive thoughts about my vision and hearing problems. What is so interesting about my volunteer job is that one of the patients, who I sometimes talk to, is totally blind. She had suffered from a real bad stroke, and she and I both talk about our struggles in trying to deal with not having good eyesight. I could just imagine what it would be like if I ever suffered from a stroke and lost my whole eyesight and was not able to see at all.

I like my job at the nursing home. I am very patient when I explain to the patients what visual and hearing impairment means to me. The numbers of the patients' rooms are right by their doors, and one good thing is the room numbers are big enough so I can read them. I get along with the patients and the nurses because they understand my disabilities, but my coworker starts freaking out at me sometimes because I cannot see or hear very well. She tries real hard to understand me, but it is very hard for us to understand one another.

I wear my glasses to help me see better. I cannot see what I am doing without my glasses and I have a hard time seeing where I am going. I got hit by a car when I was living in Davis. I was playing ball with my babysitters and some other children and I ran out into the street to try and catch the ball. At the time I was not wearing my glasses and I was not wearing a plastic shell.

I don't know how in the world I have managed to ride the taxi cab and the bus on my own for all these years. I have been thinking about how many Braille books I will read and how many braillers I will have when I become totally blind. I would still live on my own, and I would still be able to keep my apartment clean and neat, take out the garbage, do my own housework, and pay the bills. I would still be taking the van on my own to go to my volunteer job.

My visual impairments did not keep me away from being in Special Olympics. I always have to struggle and suffer from being visually and hearing impaired. I am still happy the way I am, and I am going to stay that way forever. I don't care what anyone says about my vision and hearing impairments.

I have been thinking about how old I will be if I ever

become totally blind and not be able to see ever again. I had some real bad dreams about when I went to see my eye doctor. He told me and my mom and dad that I would have to have eye surgery. In my dream, I found that after I had eye surgery and had my bad eye removed, I had gone completely blind. I have been wondering how would I feel if I ever lost all my hearing, too. It would be really hard on me and on my friends.

I have been thinking of how fun it would be for me to have my own guide dog. I would still use my white cane and I could still go out to different places with my friends and family. I have been hoping that when I become totally blind and lose my eyesight forever that people will not be afraid of me just because I cannot hear or see at all. I don't care how old I will be if something goes wrong with my eyesight. It will not matter if I am forty-five or sixty if I do become totally blind.

I was told many times, for so many years, in all of my schools and growing up with my mom and dad, that I will always still be happy. My mom did tell me that whenever someone starts making fun of me or calling me names or saying mean things because of my blindness, that I could always walk away and not pay attention to them. I have been praying real hard to god to please let me keep my eyesight in my right eye.

I had a dream a couple of nights ago, about having a stroke when I turned sixty. I dreamed that I was a patient at Woodland Hills Nursing Home. I was not able to read my menu because I was totally blind, and I had to point to each of the good foods I can eat. That was very interesting. I dreamed that my mom was the nurse's aide at the nursing home. I was in the same room as one of my patients, Valerie, is in now. I dreamed that my grandmother was my roommate.

I wish I was not visually and hearing impaired, but it is better than being totally blind and totally deaf and not be able to see and hear at all. My mother tries to make sure that people don't make fun or me or call me names. I get so tired of that. I wonder why so many people think that a person who has a vision impairment looks like a monster, with only one eye to see out of. Even some of my old friends from school have insulted me. When I was working at my old job, people would call me an ugly monster. When the girl punched me in the eye that time, I was pretty upset, but I was too afraid to tell my mom and dad what happened. But I didn't forget.

I feel like sometimes I make a fool of myself when I try to explain to people what vision and hearing impairment are all about. It is real hard for me when I get made fun of and teased or laughed at. I was told many, many times by my teachers and my family and my case counselors that it is not my fault. They say it is the other people and kids that have the problem. I wonder what I can do to explain myself better, so I won't have to make a fool of myself.

My mom told me once that I should always try and think happy thoughts. If I do ever go completely blind and I'm not able to see at all, I wonder if there is any way I will be able to explain to my friends and other people how I became visually and hearing impaired without being made fun of or laughed at.

I have been thinking about my patient Valerie. She is totally blind in both eyes. She has lots of patience with me, because she understands that I cannot see or hear very well. I do very well with my job. I know how to fix coffee for the patients at the nursing home.

TWO SIDES OF THE COIN

by Pamela Fowell

I am the parent of a child who is not only visually impaired, but also hard of hearing and congenitally challenged. While driving down the freeway recently on my way to go sailing with a group of developmentally disabled adults, some thoughts came to me about how my own experience might enlighten other parents.

The main thing I would urge is that you trust your instincts. You, more than anyone else, are the experts when it comes to your own child. Educate yourself about your child's diagnosis, but not necessarily the prognosis. Learn as much as possible about resources and support systems that may exist. Believe that love, nurturing, discipline, and the expectation for a full life will be guiding forces for your child and your family. I submit that no one knows another person's potential. Seek support for your own emotional well-being.

Take time to verbalize your darkest thoughts, feelings, fears, and concerns with your spouse and/or an experienced therapist. Be aware and thankful for the beauty of each day, for good health, for love, and for family. Give each member of your family the opportunity to express his or her own concerns, and include them in the adjustment you all must make to accept and accommodate your special needs child. Husbands and wives need to support each other so they can support their other children. Parents should be able to cry together as well as laugh together, and it should be understood that mothers and fathers frequently react very differently to the realization that their child is not, perhaps, what they expected.

Mothers and fathers would do well to respect the fact that men and women have different perspectives on parenting, or parenting a child with special needs. How women and men perceive their roles, both in marriage and with regard to their children, are often worlds apart.

The first anomaly the doctor noticed when Kimberly was born was that she had a cleft of the soft palate. We were told there might be some problems with drinking and eating, but otherwise it was not of great concern and it could be easily repaired later on. When Kim was about three weeks old, I began receiving radiation treatment for Hodgkin's Disease, which had been diagnosed during my pregnancy.

The following month we were at the doctor's office for our weekly visit. The doctor examined Kimberly's eyes and did not like what he saw. On that same day, he referred her to an opthalmologist for closer examination. When we returned to the first doctor, he told me in the kindest tone of voice he could muster that the baby girl sitting on my lap was very likely blind.

Arrangements were made for Kimberly to have a thorough eye examination, under anesthetic, at the University of California Medical Center in San Francisco. She was admitted to the Neonatal Intensive Care Unit because she was still only a few weeks old. When I took Kim into the intensive care unit I saw fragile babies in incubators as well as older, very sick children who had been hospitalized for long periods of time. I remember asking myself, "What am I doing here? My baby isn't sick."

I could see, though, that the parents who had children in the intensive care unit formed a bond of mutual caring and support with one another. It was this realization that provided the cornerstone of my strong belief in mutual support for parents of special needs children.

Kimberly was diagnosed with a complex constellation of anomalies of her eyes. She was completely blind in her left eye, had only partial vision in the right, and her eyes were severely crossed. She had abnormal cell development in the primary vitreous and a cleft in the eye structure on the globes behind her eyes. This was not the end of it, either. As the years passed we would learn of other congenital defects related to her ears and her female organs.

I continued my own radiation therapy, during which time my mother came to our house to take care of Kimberly and our five-year-old son, Jeffrey. One thing I remember vividly was the sadness I saw in my mother's face. My husband and I never talked about our thoughts or feelings regarding Kimberly and her blindness. We also avoided discussing my cancer, our son and his feelings, our relationship with each other, or our roles within the family. Each day we simply put one foot in front of the other and went on with our lives almost as if nothing had happened. It has taken me many years to realize that what happened was quite profound.

We did not blame one another, nor did we blame anyone or anything else for Kimberly's anomalies. I guess we didn't have time—or perhaps we simply didn't take time—to think about our own feelings. We had two children, a new house in the country, a garden, food to put by, jelly to make, and fruit to can for the county fair. We had a dog, cats, rabbits and chickens, and volunteer work to do at our son's school and in 4-H. While Jeff was in school, I took Kimberly everywhere I needed to go for my volunteer work, and in retrospect the older ladies I worked with were probably my first support group. Among my numerous volunteer activities, I worked with the local school district to further the Education for Handicapped Children Act. Our lives were busy and full.

Kimberly was a good baby; quiet and always seeking the light with what little vision she had. She smiled most of the time, enjoyed playing with toys and being outdoors. By two years old, though, she did not yet crawl, walk, sit up alone, make sounds, or feed herself, except for holding a bottle. We first became associated with the Blind Babies Foundation of Northern California around this time. They provided us a wonderful home counselor who guided us to specialists and resources and encouraged us to do more work with Kimberly ourselves.

Kimberly was referred to a pediatric specialist in San Francisco who disgnosed her as "significantly retarded." When my husband and I heard this we looked at each other, wondering, "What does that mean?" We were told that someday we might need to think about institutionalizing Kimberly. I recall thinking, "What on earth is this man talking about?" Kimberly's home counselor subsequently gave us several good ideas on how to work with Kim to help develop her motor skills. We never again saw the doctor who diagnosed her as retarded.

The counselor was very resourceful, and she arranged a full diagnostic work-up for Kimberly at the Diagnostic School for the Neurologically Handicapped in San Francisco. She also told us of a small pre-school for exceptional children held in a church in town. After a few months we learned of a private pre-school, also for exceptional children, that was being established in an historic rural schoolhouse not far from where we lived in the Napa Valley. The teacher was brought in by a local wealthy family who had a boy with Down Syndrome. We enrolled Kim at this school, and we found there a wonderful teacher—a Greek woman with uncanny powers of perception, the deepest caring imaginable, and extensive knowledge of special needs children and how to work with them—she was an absolute blessing in all our lives.

When Kimberly was three years old, her teacher told me she didn't think Kimberly could hear her. Another trip to U.C. Medical Center confirmed that, indeed, Kimberly could not hear and had fluid backed up behind both ears. She was pre-lingually deaf. This was the reason she could not speak. A myringotomy was performed and tubes placed in her Eustachian tubes. Kimberly soon started making sounds, and her spoken and receptive language skills progressed very rapidly. She learned to sit up by herself, and we allowed her many hours in front of the television set in order to expose her to the maximum amount of language possible.

In time, our home counselor became my mentor. I now see that my desire to work with other families and children with special needs started with our association. When Kimberly was still very young I became active with other parents of special needs children in developing a resource guide to programs, services, camps, schools, professionals, etc., in Northern California. That guide was eventually adopted by the Bay Area Board for Children with Disabilities. I collected printed information from as many sources as I could and shared them with other parents. That is something I do to this day.

Prior to her myringotomy, Kimberly had had an operation to correct her crossed eyes. By the time Kim was twelve she had been in the hospital about a dozen times for various tube placements and the reconstruction of her soft palate. Once, when Kim was seven years old, she was in the hospital for nine days. I was at her bedside the entire time.

At home, we read to Kim and provided her with stimulating toys. She was included in every aspect of our daily life. Kim started attending a summer camp for visually impaired children when she was five years old, and one year she stayed there for six weeks. She loved the camp, and we felt it was good for her to be away from the family for periods of time. She also visited her grandparents often, as they lived nearby, and Kim's aunt and cousins visited frequently, so there was considerable extended family. We also made occasional trips to Berkeley to visit her father's family.

The family's years in Napa valley, from Kimberly's birth until we moved to Davis in 1974, were very full. I worked part-time for two years after Kim started pre-school and took courses at the local community college. When Kim was quite young I felt the need for counseling, and I wanted her father to participate as well. We had friends who were involved with Synanon, a therapeutic encounter group that was popular at the time, and I decided to participate. My husband would have nothing to do with it, so I went alone, to deal with how I felt about Kimberly and about myself. I was challenged to express my innermost thoughts and feelings.

Jeff was very bright and artistic, and we decided to enroll him in a private school at age five. In retrospect, I believe he was probably too young and we should have waited until he was six before entering him in kindergarten. He was at the private school a year before going on to public school. He began having behavioral problems in about the third or fourth grade. I refused to allow him to be medicated and we shifted him to a more rural school near our home.

My husband and I attended a number of counseling sessions because of Jeff's problems. What we did not realize at the time was that Jeff was manifesting the problems his father and I were having with one another, and that our lives revolved around Kimberly. When we moved to Davis it was culture shock for Jeff, who was then entering junior high school. Davis was quite urban compared to what our environment had been in Napa.

Jeff's difficulties at school continued on and off, sometimes more seriously than others. Eventually we decided to enroll him in a private boarding school. He hated it and had a very difficult time adjusting. Adjust he did, however, and he began making good academic, social, and athletic progress. He attended for less than two years before telling us that he wanted to go back to public school. He assured us he was ready and he'd do the things he was supposed to, so we acquiesced and let him. Again, we made a mistake; he should have stayed at the boarding school.

Eventually, Jeff dropped out of high school in the eleventh grade. At one point, before he left home, he and I had a conversation about what he felt regarding Kimberly's birth defects. I learned in that conversation that he believed my cancer was the cause of her defects. I also learned that he felt left out after Kimberly was born; thus, the realization that our lives had become "about Kimberly."

I tried as lovingly as I could to assure him that I understood his feelings. I told him I was sorry we had not communicated with him better. "Communicate with Jeff ?" I think to myself now. My husband and I hardly communicated with each other, much less our children. Communication, I now believe, is a must in all families, and this is perhaps especially true in families with special needs children. Candid communication—I cannot stress it enough.

I still felt the need for counseling and participated in various types. My husband would still not attend with me. My closest friend in Davis, also the parent of a disabled child, had taken Extra Sensory Training (EST) and encouraged me to take it as well. I underwent EST, and I believe it was a good experience for me. And again, my husband would have nothing to do with it.

Kimberly attended various day schools and programs in our area. Attending admission meetings was difficult for me. Each time I needed to explain, defend, and most of all, advocate for Kim. At one such meeting I took a picture of her and passed it around the table saying that I wanted them to see the person they were going to be dealing with. I wanted them to have an association with her face and name, not just with words on paper in a folder.

On another occasion my husband and I attended a meeting in preparation for Kim to enter a new school. I remember sitting down at a huge table with perhaps a dozen people from the school district. None of them introduced themselves to me, and I never found out who they were or what any of them had to do with our daughter.

These meeting led me to be wary, and I offer the following caveat to parents of special needs children: know who all the people are at these meetings, as well as the specific purpose of the meeting. If people use unfamiliar acronyms when they talk, stop them and ask for definitions if you don't know them. Do not let professionals get away with using "educationese" with you.

When Kimberly was fourteen and about to enter junior high school, I was accepted for admission to Cal State Northridge to pursue a Special Major in the Area of the Deaf. Months of preparation and planning for leaving my family included going to counseling again. I moved to Southern California and enrolled in school on full financial aid in the fall of 1981. In 1984 my husband decided it was my turn to take care of Kimberly, so she moved to Southern California to live with me. I enrolled her in a special education high school, which she liked and where she did well. Kim was also involved in recreation programs with the Braille Institute and attended summer camp.

I finished my undergraduate degree that Spring and decided to pursue a graduate degree in Educational Psychology and Counseling with an emphasis on disabilities. Things were financially difficult that summer with no financia aidl. I eventually secured a part-time job in the dean's office, and by the following Spring my job had become full-time, so I went off financial aid and reduced my class load.

About this time, my husband moved to Southern California because he missed Kim terribly and wanted to be near her. Kim and I were both in counseling, separately but with the same person. There were times when Kim and I did not get along well, and I believe my expectations may have been too high and my patience was sometimes short. Looking back, I could have done many things differently. In retrospect, I don't think I knew how to communicate with Kimberly as well as I do now.

I was closely involved with Kim's education, and later with a program to help disabled children make the transition into society. In 1987 Kim graduated from high school, and I had a big party for her. The whole family was involved in the celebration. In the fall Kim entered an adult transition program and lived with me while doing volunteer work at

Northridge Hospital. Two years later I decided to move to the west side of Los Angeles, and Kim moved into an apartment with four other girls in the transition program.

She continued with the program and her volunteer work until the Los Angeles riots in 1992, but after that event I decided L.A. was not the place for her. I asked if she would be interested in returning to Northern California to the community living program where she had made many friends—provided, of course, that they had an opening for her. She liked the idea, so I arranged for her to have an evaluation for the program. Kim was accepted, and not long thereafter moved back to Northern California. She now shares an apartment with another girl and does volunteer work at a skilled nursing facility three days a week, which she likes very much.

Kim has her ups and downs. She is aware of things she's not supposed to do, but sometimes she rebels and does them anyway. After these episodes she says all the right things and feels bad about what happened, but there is no assurance she won't do it again. What pleases me, however, is that she can talk to me about her problems. Kim and I talk on the phone at least once a week. She says her counselor and therapist tell her the same things I do, and I continue to hope that she will be able to put into practice the good things that she knows.

Over the years I have attended innumerable conferences, workshops, and training sessions for parents of exceptional children. One time I heard a phrase that made a strong impression on me: "Parents of children with disabilities are in a perpetual state of mourning."

It is not a type of mourning that interferes with daily living, but it is subliminal and ever-present. It manifests when the parents see or feel some loss, something they missed because they are the parents of that child. I believe that having Kimberly come into my life, just the way she did, was a gift. I also believe, in spite of how strange it sounds, that having the opportunity to experience cancer was a kind of gift.

These events, and all the people that have been associated with them, have guided me to what I now consider to be the greatest gifts of my life.

PART 3
SINGLES &
SIGNIFICANT OTHERS

ON ROADS NOT TAKEN

by Jay Williams

A blind person or a person who is blind? One's perception of the degree to which blindness is a barrier and an obstacle, or just one more of life's possible glitches, depends to a large extent on whether one emphasizes the person or the disability.

I was born blind and reared by enlightened parents. They instilled in me the idea that blindness should be treated as just one of many important factors that had to be reckoned with. My life, like anyone else's, could be a success if I prepared myself well and presented a respectable persona to the world.

****

There are times when a lot of effort must be expended in order to change people's perceptions of someone with a physical disability. Unfortunately, some of those perceptions are reinforced by blind people who think the world owes them a living.

The principle obstacle in my life has always been passivity. Like Ferdinand the bull, I'm perfectly content to sit and smell the flowers. Some of this passivity was probably encouraged by the schedules at a residential school for the blind I attended. In such a Dickensian atmosphere you learn to either fight or fly. I flew away into my own world and waited for the climate to change.

I learned piano tuning and gained some musical skills. My brother tutored me in electronics, and I earned an amateur radio license. This was all very interesting, but I still had no idea what I would do with myself as a grownup. I didn't look forward to being a grownup. The majority of grownups I knew didn't seem to be having a very good time. They acted so surly and spent so much time doing things that, so far as I could tell, came to nothing.

****

I was brought up in the Midwest in the '40s and '50s. I have a generally easygoing temperament, and as a child I was inclined to go along with the prevailing beliefs and customs, no matter how much I disliked them. Luckily, a fly or two got into the ointment.

I particularly remember one midsummer's day conversation with my older brother. He was going to college in the fall and had apparently engaged in some soul-searching. Talking with me, he called into question many of the religious doctrines we had been taught. This surprised and excited me.

My brother asked me what I thought. Was I a Christian, or what? I told him I hadn't thought about it much. He proceded to berate me for my lack of integrity and impressed upon me very strongly the dangers of living without my own convictions.

"So, don't you believe any of the stuff they say in church?" I asked, a bit incredulously.

"No," he said, "but that doesn't mean you shouldn't. You have to make up your own mind."

"Then why do you go to church?"

"Same reason as you do. It's what everyone does."

A few months later my mother made a casual comment about church that really surprised me. Turns out she didn't believe any of the doctrine either. In fact, she was an orthodox atheist. Yet, during a "do's and don'ts" lecture preparatory to my leaving for college, she suggested I really should go to church.

"Huh?" I reponded.

She explained that it would help me present the kind of image our society expects.

"You gotta be kiddin'!" I thought.

****

So there I was, growing up whether I liked it or not. I vowed I would not be like all the rest of the adults I knew. At the risk of not "fitting in," I suspended my churchgoing in favor of my own concept of integrity (truth be told, I wasn't entirely unmindful of my dislike of getting up early on Sunday morning, dressing up, and putting all that goop in my hair).

In spite of nagging doubts, through my early twenties I remained pretty much resigned to the idea that my life would follow a set pattern: get the appropriate degrees, get a middling teaching position, and eventually raise a family. Yawn.

Then came a real awakening. I discovered modern classical music. I got my master's degree in music from Indiana University and applied for teaching jobs. In the name of integrity, I wrote "blindness" in the box on the application that asked about physical handicaps. And on those applications that included space for a brief essay, I always wrote something to the effect of: "Since I am blind, my natural reliance on sound makes me well suited for..."

Welcome to the real world! It didn't take long before I saw a curious pattern begin to emerge: I would get a letter from college X informing me the job was filled, and the same day a friend from my master's program would get a letter from the same college thanking him for his application and stating that the decision was still pending. I was finally granted an interview at a small liberal arts college, but two days before I was to go there, I got a call from the department head. I was told: "We've looked over your application again, and, well, I'm afraid your handicap would cause us more problems than we can handle."

"Well, then, who's handicapped?" I asked before slamming the receiver down as hard as I could. Never mind that I had nearly a 4.0 grade point average and teaching experience as a graduate assistant. And here I thought music was the art of the ear, not the eye. Needless to say, I was angry, but I had to admit that integrity didn't presume naiveté.

I went back to school and began to work toward a doctorate. After a year or so I met up with some of my friends who had gotten those teaching jobs. Most of them were changed people. Where was all that zeal and lightness of spirit I had known? Their descriptions of their work were not encouraging. I became convinced that for the time being, I didn't belong in that kind of position after all.

The following year an electronic music studio opened at the university, and it didn't take long to realize I had found my niche. I decided to stick around and compose electronic music. A famous avant-garde composer was hired to administer the new program, and I was hired along with four other students to teach the courses. I also became the university's piano technician. I found that the combination of flexible hours and working to unlock the mysteries of piano innards agreed with me.

****

Then came the cultural changes of the late '60s. Suddenly, "different was beautiful." It was a time when many of us began to ask ourselves those "know thyself" questions, and it dawned on me that the greatest barriers in my life resulted from my willingness to let chance circumstances rule my thinking and behavior. I had been asleep at the wheel for too long. It was time to make my own decisions rather than "blindly" follow a path prescribed by others. I resolved to do things according to my own ideals.

Now, nearly three decades later, my life runs at a pace I

am comfortable with. It continues to be the kind of adventure I have always wanted.

BARRIERS OR BUILDING BLOCKS?

Kathy Seven Williams

It amazes me that I have had such a block over writing this piece. At every start I would run headlong into such emotional resistance. I felt I was getting nowhere. I protested to myself that I hadn't had a life filled with barriers. But a promise is a promise. I said I would write, and so I will.

The main point I want to get across is how equal I have felt throughout my life. I believe the barriers I met and overcame were no higher or tougher than anyone else's.

Were they different from the barriers most people encounter? Some were, some weren't. If I were pressed to objectivity, I'd say most were due, at least to some degree, to my low vision. But if I were forced to place the blame somewhere, I would have to blame my lack of patience, my quick tongue, my frustration with stupidity, and my sense of caring for my fellow man. With that said...

****

When I was three years old my mother, my sister, and I came to California to find a new and better life after Mom's divorce. When it came time for me to enter the first grade—or so the story goes—Mom was told I needed to go to the State School for the Blind. She insisted, however, that I didn't need to be institutionalized.

State law called for a resource room—equipped with Braille books, Braille typrwriters, tapes, etc.—in the local school district. Mom rounded up eleven blind or partially sighted kids, and the school district kept its end of the bargain by finding us a resource teacher. The children came from several surrounding communities, arriving by car, taxicab, and minibus. We made use of the resource room from first through eighth grade, but at the same time we were mainstreamed—that is, included in the general classrooms with the sighted students—and encouraged to solve our own problems. At the end of junior high school we dispersed, but all of the students in my class eventually graduated from their own neighborhood schools.

Were there barriers in elementary and junior high school? I wouldn't say so. There was, however, the never-ending problem of physical education. I used to hide in the bathroom so I wouldn't have to go out into that hateful sunshine, where my vision became almost nil and my sense of self-control and direction became terribly confused. I once taught the class to play Steal the Bacon, a kind of relay game that I could make sense of and compete in without seeing what was actually happening. Even so, I hated P.E., but the students didn't seem to notice. I could shoot baskets and catch the ball on the rebound by sound. I pitched a great game of softball, sitting down after each pitch to avoid the returning ball and letting the shortstop step up and cover my spot for fielding. The worst part of elementary and junior high school was probably the fact that I was bussed there, so I had relatively few chances to play with friends after school and on weekends.

In high school there seemed to be hardly any barriers related to my blindness. I was the school's first blind student, so we worked out accommodations together as the need arose. School came so easily to me that it seemed I hardly had to work at it to do well. I could read if I had to, nose pressed to book, at about half an hour per page. I passed tests successfully by listening closely in class. I also took copious notes in a clear, legible hand. I had no way of reading them myself, but friends would read them aloud to me in return for getting to use the information themselves. I think it was partly the carefully taught handwriting that made it so easy for me to fit in at school without any special help.

I was assigned to a daily study hall. This is where I met all the "hoods" of the school, since they were the only other students to be confined to study hall. This could have been a major problem, but I taught them all Braille, drawn in ballpoint pen on notebook paper, and this provided them with a language none of the teachers could decipher.

One of the "hoods" had his locker next to mine, and I remember how he used to walk up and see me struggling with my combination. He would say, "Get back" and then he would kick the locker in just the right spot, popping it open for me. He'd never say another word to me anywhere on campus, but he always took care of that one little problem for me.

At graduation, by luck of the draw, I found myself walking in next to one of these "hoods." Outdoors, where I had difficulty seeing in the bright sunlight, he simply and silently offered me his elbow in proper and untaught sighted-guide technique and showed me to my row. I released his arm, and we completed the ceremony without another word.

****

I remember going to the chemistry lab the summer before my senior year in high school to speak with the teacher. I told him that I wanted to take chemistry and I needed to talk with him about some of the things we might have to deal with on account of my blindness. He walked over to a lab table, turned on a Bunsen burner, and asked, "Can you see that?" I could see there was something moving against the black lab table, but I didn't know what it was.

"Can you see the flame?" he asked.

"What flame?" I replied.

"I don't ever want to see you in this lab again," he said. And that was the end of chemistry.

I took physics instead and loved every minute of it. Each lab lecture was made wonderfully clear to me through creative teaching and hands-on demonstrations. I think if magnified reading machines for the blind had come along five years earlier I'd have become a physicist.

****

The most peculiar form of discrimination toward me came as a result of the dark glasses I always wore. I was born with no cones in my retinas, and I am extremely sensitive to light of any kind. For that reason, I wore the darkest sunglasses possible in order to see anything at all in the sunlight. (I could see pretty well in the dark, though, beating my good sport of a father at badminton every game.)

Because of my dark glasses, the campus cop apparently mistook me for a druggie—these were the '60s, after all, and drugs were not uncommon around the campus. I remember once the cop taunted me by singing the Batman theme song. I related this to the principal and asked him to explain to the policeman the error of his ways. I must confess, though, to taking advantage of his subsequent embarrassment by more than once leaving campus early without question or restraint.

****

One of my favorite phrases is, "You've got to be taught," from the song of the same name in the musical South Pacific. I was always taught that there is nothing I cannot do, and that "can't" is a foreign concept. It was up to me to find a way to succeed in anything I tried.

Driver's education was a legal requirement for graduation from high school in California. I not only took the class, but I earned an A. On the final day of class, when everyone went out to the parking lot to take the driving test, I was shocked to find out I wouldn't be taking that part of the course. It may sound funny, but I think that was the first time I realized that blindness could be an actual barrier, and that "blind" meant "different from my peers." Until then, no one had ever suggested to me that there were limits to what I could do (notwithstanding the stubborn chemistry professor). To this day, I wonder if I wouldn't do as well as a lot of others out there on the roads, but whenever I fail to see a car merging in front of us or a pedestrian walking in the middle of the street, that assures me I really had better not try.

****

There were good and bad things about being one of the few mainstreamed blind kids in California moving on to college. I had been taught to solve my own problems and forge my own path, and I had become a bright and enthusiastic student. I was also, I can see now, a bit arrogant. For example, when someone asked me why I had applied to Swarthmore, my reply was, "As backup in case I don't get into U.C. Santa Cruz."

I ended up enrolling at U.C. Riverside, but with four years of A's in high school French already under my belt, I undertook a year of remedial study in French at Riverside and transferred to McGill University in Montreal as a French major for my sophomore year. I lived in a French dorm, speaking fractured French, and at the end of my first semester I earned a D-minus.

The main problem was that I couldn't see the test papers. My professor's response, though, was that I had no business being there. Well, perhaps I didn't. I changed my major to sociology, and shortly thereafter switched again, this time to English. But the problem with reading continued to dog me. Finally I hit on a new strategy. A tour through the college bookstore yielded the class major with the fewest books, and I became a psychology major.

I transferred to a small private college, where I mustered up the courage to stand up in front of the class and ask for readers, whom I offered to pay $2.65 per hour for reading what they would have to read for the class anyway. That's how I found Doug. He was the best reader I'd ever had—and thirty years later he still is. Doug read everything for me, from astronomy to Mark Twain, and got me through the next three-and-a-half years to my B.A. in psychology. I had a couple of other exceptional readers as well, including Linda, who could read in fast forward, never missing a syllable.

There were two teachers in particular who tested me verbally instead of in writing (oddly enough, they both taught science). My biology teacher, for example, decided that instead of painstakingly describing each drawing and diagram on the final exam, he would simply ask me what grade I thought I'd earned. I told him, honestly, I felt, that I'd earned a B-plus, and that's exactly what he gave me. In the lab, he made sure I had the chance to dissect everything the other students did, although he kindly excused me—along with a few other overly sensitive students—from having to participate in the vivisection of a rat. I remember the experience of seeing the division of cells in a sea urchin's egg through an electron microscope set to very high contrast.

The only near-disaster was my abnormal psychology class, which was required for my major. The course was taught by a man who told me very bluntly that women did not belong in college and blind women in particular belonged in institutions. He even refused to give me a final examination. The department chair agreed to read me the final, question by question, asking me to type the answers on his office typewriter. I earned an A, and in so doing I also earned the respect of the difficult professor. I had always considered the problem to be his barrier, not mine; as things turned out, I was able to show him a way around it.

****

My first job out of college was a position as an assistant to the director of special student services at a community college. My boss, who used a wheelchair, taught me everything I ever wanted to know about access and affirmative action. Wherever we traveled, one or the other of us would check public toilets for accessibility.

Low vision can be a curse, though, as well as a blessing. For example, blind people cannot always recognize others by voice alone. I am able to see hairstyles, patterns on clothing, and some other details, but I cannot see facial features or colors. One time, while I was attending a meeting of the governor's Committee on Employment of the Handicapped, I met all sorts of government and industry bigwigs. They seemed amazed by my ability to recognize both them and their professional connections. The next day, however, I was out of luck. I had managed to recognize them the day before largely by the look of their ties, and now their ties had all been changed.

****

I have held a variety of jobs, received computer training, and educated myself to become a specialist in serving the blind and low vision community. I have also experienced three marriages, two children, and a move from California to Utah that I consider to be a mixed blessing. But these are the subjects of another book. The most important thing I can emphasize here is that my life continues to move forward. I am now heavily involved with the Internet, specifically in providing access to information for everyone who wants it. The same way I sign off my e-mail, I will sign off here:

Helen Keller wrote: "While they were saying among themselves it cannot be done, it was done."

Keep doing it.

MARCHING FORWARD

by Mike Hoenig

"He is blind."

This was the verdict my parents received from doctors at University Hospitals in Iowa City six months after my birth. While still coping with the initial shock of this news, they began—like so many other parents in such a situation—to ask, "What next?"

Blindness was something new to my family. Neither of my parents attended high school, both having spent virtually their whole lives on rural Iowa farms. They compensated for their lack of book learning with unconditional love, common sense, and the sincere desire to include me in all aspects of family life.

My parents spent the first years of my life catering to my every whim. At age three, I was still being fed and dressed. I had to undergo periodic tests and evaluations concerning my blindness and, at the end of one grueling day of medical assessment, the various professionals at the hospital called us all together for a conference.

"How is Mike?" asked my father.

"Mike is fine," came the reply. "The parents are the ones who have the problem."

From that day forward, I was made to feed and dress myself. I initially didn't take too kindly to this change, telling my parents that if they would not feed me, I'd just starve. Soon, though, I managed to reassume my position as "king of the castle." My eldest sister, who had already left home, frequently came to visit, lavishing me with gifts and kind words. My other sister, then in high school, couldn't do enough for me. If on a rare occasion my parents did not comply with my wishes, I needed only to run to her in order to get my way.

My mother had a wonderful talent for teaching me things. One of my very earliest memories is sitting on the floor with her, learning to spell using large plastic letters and a magnetic board. I always enjoyed "helping" her make cookies and brownies. One of the first times I remember exercising my independence was my attempt to make brownies at age four. The kitchen was a disaster when I finished, but I was praised, not punished. My family knew I would have to learn by experience.

At age five I had an IQ test and was told I was very smart. I was enrolled in the Iowa Braille and Sight Saving School in Vinton, Iowa, a place I would call home for the better part of the next eleven years. My first two years at Vinton were probably the most difficult of my entire life. I felt as though my family had been taken away from me, and I didn't feel any more special than anyone else. Suddenly I had to make my own way.

The idea of traveling alone from one destination to another was frightening to me. I was a good student, but I had no idea how to socialize with my peers. To borrow a line from Dickens, "I felt quite alone in the world." Yet, even at such a young age, I never questioned that my parents were doing the best thing for me.

Things began to change during my third year at the school. I discovered my sense of humor, and I also found that popularity was somehow linked to being a prankster. Though the teachers weren't always appreciative of my antics, I got away with more than I should have because they saw me coming out of my shell. I was starting to socialize with others for the first time.

The next several years were generally happy ones. I enjoyed school, and I was very pleased when a home bussing program was instituted. This meant a guarantee of going home to visit my family at least once every three weekends.

Summers, I remember, were glorious times, filled with fishing adventures, baseball games, card games with my family, and trips to see friends. Whatever our family did, I was a part of it.

It was around that time that I began to understand just how fortunate I was to have a supportive, understanding family. I loved swimming and my mom took me a lot. One day, as I was preparing to go to the pool, my mother suggested I call another blind student who lived nearby to see if he could come too. I called him several times, but inevitably his mother would find an excuse for his not being able to go. Every visit to his home found him listening to talking books in his hot, tiny bedroom.

During summer vacation of my freshman year in high school, our local baseball team advanced to the state tournament. This was an exciting time for me, and it marked my first real interaction with sighted peers. Even though they were close to my own age, I idolized them.

High school became a wonderful time in my life. Yes, I had all the "problems" any adolescent experiences, but I felt I had the world by the tail. I held class office each year, I had a girlfriend and I played in the school band. I even started to excel in sports, and I always maintained a solid grade point average.

During my senior year the school tried an experiment. We were placed in the Vinton public high school for one or two periods each school day. I was terrified. In the public school classroom, my bold, gregarious self shrunk into a timid child who spoke only when directly addressed. I remember how excited I was the first time another student spoke to me.

A psychology class during my second semester gave me my first taste of discrimination. I was placed in the class with a partially sighted classmate, and while it seemed he was readily welcomed by the teacher and the other students, I felt shunned. Looking back, it was probably a good experience, as it forced me to assert myself as someone worthy of respect.

College presented another challenging transition. I distinctly remember wishing for a tornado or some other tragedy to strike the night prior to my leaving for school. Again, the unknown....

Settling into the academic routine was actually much easier than I'd expected. I quickly found readers, and I felt very much at ease. When necessary, I made alternate test-taking arrangements with extremely cooperative professors.

Social life, though, was another matter. The shift from a close-knit, sheltered environment to the outside world seemed almost unbearable. For nearly the entire first year of college, I yearned to return home.

I remember on the last night of my freshman year, I pressed a fellow student into emergency duty and had him read me a Spanish exam. We began to talk after the test was done and realized we'd been experiencing many of the same feelings about life. He was an African American in a predominantly white community; I was a blind person in a predominantly sighted world.

Our friendship grew during my sophomore year, and suddenly college life seemed to open up for me. I joined several clubs, I truly enjoyed the concert band, and I even talked the director into letting me be a part of the college marching band. She had concerns about my marching and playing at the same time, so she offered me a position on the flag line. I spent a semester in the Yucatan, another as a practicum student, and I joined a fraternity. Through all this, I came to realize for the first time that I didn't need to idolize all my sighted peers. I felt I had achieved complete acceptance from the sighted world when a college friend, upon learning that we would both be graduate students at the University of Iowa the next year, asked me to share an apartment.

I gained even more confidence from the training I received at the Iowa Department for the Blind from their Adult Orientation Center. Until then, the mere thought of boiling water—let alone cooking a full meal—had always terrified me. So had traveling alone in a large metropolitan area. As I first managed to boil water, then cook pork chops on my own, I started to believe that I really could be independent.

My fears about traveling alone were forever put to rest during that first summer at the Center. I remember, at the end of a particularly frustrating day when nothing seemed to go right, the teacher asked me, "Did you learn anything?" When I said that I had, she assured me the day had not been wasted, that it was perfectly fine to make mistakes along the way.

We spent considerable time discussing the importance of setting straight the prevalent public attitudes about blindness. I'd had very little exposure to discriminatory attitudes, and I wondered if the people at the Department for the Blind weren't getting us "all worked up" over nothing.

I got the answer to that question shortly thereafter, when I moved into the Iowa City apartment. Our landlady seemed only to be able to deal with my sighted roommate, and things changed only after she and I sat down for a frank discussion. I explained that I was competent and I wanted to be treated equally. In retrospect, I'm glad I got "all worked up."

I think my growing self-sufficiency was difficult for my parents at first. I will always remember a visit home during my junior year in college, when we got into a heated discussion about family finances. My dad said he was bequeathing more money to me than to my sisters, and when I asked why, he responded, "Because they can see."

Later on, as we discussed the future, Dad said to me, "After college you can live at home and play the piano part-time at the nursing home." Though probably quite unintentionally, at that moment he motivated me to prove that I could be a productive, successful adult. I began doing just that in 1985, when I was hired as a rehabilitation teacher with the state Department for the Blind in Des Moines. I learned later of the fear my parents had about my living alone, but at the time they supported and encouraged me as I ventured forth.

My three-and-a-half years at the Department were challenging and extremely time-intensive. I was assigned anywhere from fifteen to thirty counties, forcing me to quickly learn the techniques of good time management. As I traveled from home to home with a driver, I also got a few lessons in managing other people, including the experience of firing an employee.

I also learned to empathize with people who had lost their eyesight later in life. On reflection, I feel sorry for those first few clients I had who spoke to a very unsympathetic ear about the challenges of blindness. I'd met those challenges just fine, so why couldn't they? When I finally realized that a big part of my job was to listen to what others had to say, I began to understand what it must be like to lose something you've taken for granted your whole life. You might be surprised how often this lesson still benefits me.

In 1989 I accepted a teaching post with the Illinois Department of Rehabilitation and moved to the Quad City area (as the four cities of Rock Island and Moline, IL; and Bettendorf and Davenport, IA, are collectively known). Unfortunately, it soon became apparent that my teaching philosophy and that of the department were not compatible. Less than a year into the job, with the prospect of my own firing looming, I accepted a position with the newly established Center for Independent Living.

Centers, as they are commonly called, are non-profit organizations, usually operating on limited resources. I had to take a drop in pay when I switched jobs, but this was more than compensated for by the fast-paced, interesting work. I had the opportunity to instruct and really help blind individuals in various activities of daily living. I also began to attend community meetings on topics of my interest, such as transportation.

Within six months I was promoted to Director of Programs, a position I held for more than three years. It was during this time that I took an interest in community activism. I ran and was elected to local and then state boards; it made me feel proud and grateful to learn that people felt I had valuable things to say.

It was around that time that I began puzzling over something that I'm unsure of to this day—determining when to call attention to my disability, and when to accept a situation as being a natural part of everyday life. Many of my colleagues in the Independent Living movement were holding public demonstrations, demanding the assistance they needed to be independent in the community. I didn't feel comfortable with that kind of confrontational style, but I did recognize that enormous work needs to be done in order to make the world more accessible to people with all types of disabilities.

In late 1992 I remarked to my boss, "I wish there were a job that was all advocacy and no managing of other employees." I recall feeling prophetic a short while later when a friend called from the University of Iowa to tell me he was writing a grant that, if funded, would provide special training to Iowans with disabilities. The project would need a director. Was I interested?

The grant was approved, and I was hired in September 1993. It has been as close to a perfect fit as employee and employer could hope for. Even the two-hour daily commute, which many people find daunting, offers me a welcome opportunity to read and relax. I have to transfer from a special paratransit van to a university van, but for the first time in my working life I don't have to brave the cold while waiting for a city bus.

Sometimes I find it ironic that I frequently speak to groups of disabled people about their rights, yet I'm not entirely sure myself what rights I feel the need to exercise. For instance, if I am staying at a hotel and find no tactile markings on the doors, do I talk to the management about the requirement for such markings under the Americans With Disabilities Act, or do I take pride in managing just fine without them? Do I prefer to attend a play that offers an audio accompaniment, calling attention to my blindness, or do I simply blend in with the crowd and miss out on critical information?

Lest I create the impression that life is just a big question mark for me, let me share with you some Facts According to Hoenig:

Fact 1. A blind person, if he or she chooses, can do just about anything a sighted person can do. The caveat? It often takes a whole lot more time, patience, and work to accomplish it. I will illustrate by sharing one or two experiences.

In 1988 a friend told me about a two-week travel study program to the Soviet Union. My boss graciously gave me the time with pay, and plans proceeded quite smoothly. But that all changed when the tour sponsor learned I was blind. Suddenly the rules were changed, and I was required to have a companion in order to attend the program. After many letters and phone calls, I finally pursuaded them to let me make the trip.

Before leaving I called up my pre-assigned roommate, and when I told him he would be rooming with a blind person, he said, "I'm delighted!" He began sending me Russian language tutorial tapes, and by the time we met in New York City, I felt like we'd been friends for years. In the end, I had a wonderful and enriching trip to the Soviet Union.

Since that time I've faced numerous similar experiences. One cruise line insisted that I sign a waiver of liability, backing down only when I produced legal papers from the Civil Rights Commission. Recently, a tour director I was dealing with had to give "considerable thought" to whether having an unaccompanied blind person along was a good idea. So far, though, I've never been denied access to a trip, and I have found each and every experience worthwhile.

I was pleased last year when I met no resistance whatsoever in planning a trip to New Zealand. I put the trip together with the help of New Zealand colleagues, who saw absolutely no reason why I shouldn't travel there. The "Kiwis," as they call themselves, got it right. Perhaps their American counterparts will someday follow suit.

Fact 2. Whether or not we choose to accept the charge, blind people are teachers during our every waking moment.

The wedding rehearsal had ended. The groom's mother approached a group of us and said, "All right, all you men can start stacking the chairs." Wanting to help, I reached for a chair, only to be thwarted by her. "I really didn't mean you," she explained. "Last I checked I was still a man," I replied. I believe my friend's mother learned something that day, as she has never again suggested that I refrain from joining in on account of my blindness.

I was enjoying lunch with a friend recently when I overheard a very proper English accent at the next table say, "Look. He's putting sour cream on his potato. Isn't it marvelous?" Very calmly, I turned toward the voice and said, "I've had lots of practice." There were no more comments about my eating prowess, but as we got up to leave, the lady addressed my friend and said, "Tell him he does so well." He immediately replied, "You tell him." To her credit, she did so, and we soon lapsed into conversation about a common acquaintance. She and I maintain contact to this day. Another lesson learned.

Fact 3. Having a sense of humor is absolutely essential.

Several years ago, I was asked to be a temporary counselor at a camp for adults with severe disabilities. I was told that Martin, the person for whom I would be responsible, was self-sufficient; I would need only to provide minimal supervision. Though a man of very few words, Martin proved to be utterly delightful—that is, until it came time to retire to the tent for the evening. To my dismay, he required a great deal of help with every aspect of getting ready for bed, and he needed an equal amount of help when we arose early the next morning. The pattern continued for the rest of the week.

The following year at the same camp, I was assigned to Don. Don, I was told, was just as self-sufficient as Martin. "Oh, no..." I thought as we went to the tent. And sure enough, it was Martin all over again. Then, just as Don was ready to struggle into his sleeping bag, a counselor from the next tent hollered to me, "Hey, Mike, can I borrow a flashlight?"

My jaw dropped in astonishment. I was blind—of course I didn't have a flashlight. Hadn't had one last year either. That's when I realized that neither Martin nor Don had the intellectual capacity to tell me they needed light to do all the things I do routinely in the dark. After a moment of silent embarrassment, I started to laugh.

Fact 4. Blind people have the same hopes, dreams, trials, and successes as sighted people.

If you take nothing else from this story, please remember that last sentence. Far too often, sighted people erroneously assume that physical blindness alone sets a blind person apart from society. Not so. I am a wage-earner, a die-hard St. Louis Cardinals fan, and an aficionado of ragtime music. I own my home, I have a religious preference, and I wonder what will happen when my eighty-six-year-old father can no longer drive.

Sound familiar? It should. I may use Braille to balance my checkbook, but at the end of the month it's balanced. I may have to walk on the flag line in the college marching band, but I'm still in the band. And you may need light to do things I can do perfectly well in the dark. So I say to sighted and blind readers alike, let us accept and appreciate one another's differences, enjoy our commonalities, and march through life together.

NEW PERSPECTIVES

by Lance Dawson

My childhood in the mid-1960s was not easily distinguishable from that of the average boy. I engaged in the same activities as any other young lad. I was no worse than most, and in some ways I was perhaps better behaved. In fact, one might say my childhood was unremarkable, with one exception: I had to pee all the time.

My life was like one-half of the old saying; I just wasn't full of vinegar. Even the oblivious nature of a nine-year-old can be jarred by several trips to the boys' room during the school day, followed by several more during the night. I remember with what trepidation I mentioned this condition to my parents, and with what self-importance I entered the hospital for a three-day diagnostic visit. At the end of those three days, I learned I had diabetes.

Diabetes? What did that mean? For me it meant two shots of self-injected insulin every day. That meant no spending the night away from home, no days without checking blood sugar levels, and no eating birthday cake. (What? No birthday cake? Well, no sweets in front of the folks.) As a result of this dietary regimen, coupled with the way my body metabolized sugar, I grew up very slender. Even being thin, however, a boy can be downright cool as a diabetic. "That's right," I would boast to my friends, "I give myself two shots a day!" Imagine how heroic that sounded to my prepubescent peers. My nonchalance with the disease lasted about fifteen years. No one ever told me diabetes was a leading cause of blindness.

The vision loss didn't happen overnight. I was twenty-four years old, working as a waiter and part-time disc jockey, when I noticed a small, dark, wormlike thread in my field of vision. A "floater," the opthalmologist called it. Incredulous, I listened to what else he had to say.

"We're in trouble, Lance," he continued. I deduced that this actually meant I was in trouble. Several dozen laser treatments and three surgeries over the next thirteen months proved to be no match for Mr. Diabetes. I clearly remember the doctor saying, "I'm sorry, Lance, there's nothing more we can do." The one thing I can't recall is the look on his face; I was twenty-five years old, and I was totally blind.

Blind. My tendency toward optimism hadn't allowed me to believe it would ever come to this. But it was true. Not only could I no longer see, I couldn't read, write, or travel. (I suppose I actually could write, just not legibly; but to be honest, I couldn't write legibly even when I was able to see.) My mind raced with all the things I could no longer do. But one day of that negativity was all my sunny disposition could take. I decided, first things first: I needed to learn to get around. My life was about to start over again—my new life with a new perspective on the world.

Mobility issues were my initial concerns. My world consisted of only darkness, and I had to learn to get around somehow. Ladies and gentlemen! Allow me to introduce: mobility through cane work! The usefulness of a white cane for a blind individual's mobility cannot be overstated. The initial awkwardness in using a cane soon gave way to total dependence on this invaluable tool. New skills became equivalent with successful travel. These skills included such things as recognizing tactile changes in the pavement and awareness of auditory clues, like running water or wind chimes. Even the sun assisted in the learning process, becomming a directional marker instead of the light source it had always been.

Before long, unaccompanied travel no longer provoked terror, only a modest anxiety. Now the terror belonged to those who shared the sidewalk with me as I wielded this new weapon. Moses parting the Red Sea had nothing over a resolute blind person with a wildly arcing white cane.

Once I understood the basic requirements for mobility, reading and writing were next in line, and Braille seemed the appropriate response to the challenge. The downside with Braille is not the difficulty: only ten patterns need to be memorized to effectively use grade-one Braille. The problem is the sheer volume of information: a Braille dictionary runs about twenty-three volumes. Exacerbating my trouble reading Braille was my neuropathy—a fancy way of saying nerve damage—which caused a lack of sensation in my feet and fingertips. This was another lovely parting gift from my diabetes. Nevertheless, I used the language of raised dots to label my food cans at home. I wished to avoid as many nights of "chef's surprise" as possible. You haven't lived until you've had a good steaming can of fruit cocktail.

After achieving some semblance of security in my darkness, I encountered a problem over which I had very little control (or so I thought at the time). This problem was people's perception of me as a blind individual. As a rule, I now say "an individual who is blind." In so doing, the emphasis is placed on the person rather than the disability. Terrific... if only I had felt that way then. I decided I was now defined primarily as someone who could not see. But it didn't take long for me to realize that problems ache for solutions, and I had the ability to resolve this one. Attitudes can, and usually do, correlate with changes in perception. Clearly, I needed to raise the comfort level of those near me. After personally accepting my blindness and achieving some degree of comfort with my disability, I decided others should be comfortable around me as well.

I found that humor was a perfect comfort elixir. It worked like a charm. Laughter at awkward moments, self-deprecating remarks, even blind jokes—whatever it took to lighten the atmosphere—became fixtures in my interactions. (For Halloween I would dress as a pirate with patches over both eyes.) I noticed changes in peoples' attitude and behavior almost immediately. People no longer seemed to define me solely by my disability, but judged me by personality. As long as I didn't behave like a helpless, pitiable waif, I wouldn't be treated like one.

Lest you become swayed by my angelic behavior toward my fellow human beings, I must admit I have had moments of devilish shame. I once was handed a Braille menu in a restaurant, and upon the waiter's return, I exclaimed that the menu was in Spanish. Of course, I couldn't actually read the menu at all, but I delighted in the waiter's embarrassment. What do you think of my halo now?

Honestly, though, I'm not sure I should bear the full weight of responsibiity for such foolishness. Truth be told, I all too often encounter behavior that cannot help but drive my actions in such sadistic directions. You'd be amazed by the number of people who raise their voices when speaking to me. I'm not hard of hearing, I'm hard of seeing. Another example: I may take your arm for assistance getting across a busy intersection, but I do not need to be propped up against a wall to keep from falling down; I can actually stand up without the use of a scaffold, kickstand, or flying buttress.

While I'm in the middle of ranting, if you need information from me, just ask me. Do not ask my companion what I would like to order for lunch, or where it hurts. I'll show you where it hurts. Just promise me two things: First, treat me with the same respect, dignity and courtesy as you would anyone else; no more, no less. Second, do not hesitate to offer assistance; just be certain it is accepted before the laying on of hands. This last request is a recommended practice when interacting with anyone who is visibly disabled.

While the perceptions and behaviors of others continue to be largely beyond my control, my own perceptions of the world will always be formed by my own definitions. True, I am comfortable with the state of my existence, but that level of comfort does not necessarily equate to a similar level of satisfaction. It took me quite some time to develop an appreciation for what may seem like a sad situation.

Whether we are willing to admit it, we are all influenced by aesthetic prejudices. Clothing, automobiles, homes, and, unfortunately, friends, all fall subject to the whims of fancy and fashion. As the saying goes, beauty is in the eye of the beholder, but ugly is hard to stomach.

With the onset of my blindness, suddenly there were no more ugly-looking people in my life. In all seriousness, I began to wonder just how many truly fascinating people had escaped my attention due strictly to my own aesthetic prejudices. How dreadfully simple-minded of me! After missing out on innumerable remarkable conversations as a result of fashion choices or bouffant hairdos that I didn't happen to go for, my vision loss affords me the opportunity to never again prematurely forgo social interactions due to appearance.

This is not to suggest that because I can no longer make those snap judgments, I automatically enjoy a lively and fulfilling life without sight. There are a number of bonuses, strictly for the visually impaired, that simplify or improve our existence. No one asks you to drive them to the airport, and you are never called upon to be the designated driver. You are never expected to pick out a Valentine's Day card for your Aunt Louise. I could enumerate a long list of such examples, but these will suffice for now.

Overall, society's expectations of the blind are greatly reduced. This can, of course, be immensely frustrating. Legitimate pride for an accomplished task is offset, often as not, by some well-intentioned praise for going to the bathroom unaccompanied. Nevertheless, one must be willing to admit that when the bar of expectation is lowered, the probability of success increases. I am not suggesting, nor do I condone, a lack of effort in any undertaking by a person with vision loss. For me, the most incredible thing about losing my sight occured with the realization that its effect on my life was relatively marginal. Imagine my satisfaction in graduating as university valedictorian, marrying the person of my dreams, and finding a rewarding vocation, all without the use of a key sense such as eyesight.

The whole is much greater than the sum of its parts. Consequently, the removal of one of those parts—eyesight, for example—does not render the subject diminished in any way. I may have lost my sight, but I'm still the same person. My efforts and activities after losing my eyesight include skydiving, kayaking in the Pacific, riding horseback in Mexico, skiing, snowmobiling, and even jetskiing. Before losing my sight I could get winded just looking for the remote control.

So often when tragedy strikes there is a tendency to ask, "Why me?" I have also asked this question, but my experience as an individual who is blind continues to prove fulfilling, rewarding, and enlightening. Do I actually believe my life has improved since I became blind? Maybe. It all depends on one's perspective. Perhaps I should say it all depends on how one views the world. The accomplishments, relationships, and revelations from my loss of eyesight and the necessary adjustments have proven to be both challenging and rewarding. This realization brings me to a single final thought: In spite of the problems confronting humanity, the world and all it holds looks pretty good to me.

FADING SIGHT

by Tania Gregory

I remember my first experience with night blindness, when I was five years old. It was Halloween, and I wanted to dress up as a ghost. My mother fashioned me a costume out of an old bed sheet, and with my plastic pumpkin in hand, I left at dusk with my father. It wasn't even all that dark outside, but even so I walked right off a neighbor's porch into their juniper bushes.

My father thought maybe the eyeholes of my costume had been cut too small, but even after he ripped them to about the size of Montana, I saw nothing. I peered out into the darkness, barely able to see what my little flashlight fell upon.

Imagine growing up unable to function normally in low-level lighting. Add to that a slowly narrowing visual field. Forget driving at night, or driving at all. I dreaded high school dances and walking out to a date's car after a football game. Nightclubs were out of the question, and locating someone in a restaurant or darkened room was virtually impossible. I couldn't read name tags at functions, and in a theater it was unthinkable to get up in the middle of a movie to use the bathroom.

****

My night blindness is a huge social obstacle, and no amount of carrots, beta carotene, or Chinese acupuncture can cure it. People are forever asking me, "Wouldn't a stronger glasses perscription help?" A friend from college even offered to lend me his glasses, thinking that would do the trick. Don't people think I would use any means possible if I thought it would improve my sight? People who don't know me might think I am stuck-up or obnoxious because I frequently don't acknowledge handshakes. It's frustrating because at first glance it doesn't appear as though anything is wrong with me; that is, until I trip over a fire hydrant in broad daylight.

****

Eye doctors were stumped as to why I could not see in the dark and why my visual acuity was below normal. I received a formal diagnosis of retinitis pigmentosa in 1992, but I remained above the level of legal blindness until I was in graduate school. My eyesight was not bad enough until then to receive significant attention from anyone, including myself.

It was not until I moved to San Francisco from the East Coast that I learned to use a white cane—something that had once been inconceivable. Because my depth perception had been significantly reduced, it was difficult for me to discern steps or curbs. And because I had lost almost all of my peripheral vision, I needed the cane to alert others that I might not be able to see them.

Picking up and using a white cane was one of the hardest things I have ever done. Cane technique is not complicated; the hard part was accepting the fact that I needed it. Intellectually, I knew I needed to use a cane, but I was afraid of it. The very idea of a cane crushed me. I hated it. I knew I would be safer, more independent, and would end up with fewer bruises on my shins; nevertheless, it embarrassed me. I was afraid people would feel sorry for me, pity me, or think I was somehow a diminished person. It took a long time for me to walk down the street using my cane and not feel like everyone was talking about me. I had to get over myself.

If I am in a familiar place during the daytime, I can pass

as someone with normal sight. I will use my cane to cross the street, then fold it up and go into a department store or the office where I work. I know the time may come when cane use will no longer be an option but a necessity for me.

It is exhausting for me to rely solely on what remains of my vision to maneuver through the world. After a long day at work, when I've been using my eyes all day at the computer and looking through case files, the cane makes it easier for me to get home. It reduces my stress levels and gives my overworked eyes a rest.

I now accept my need for the cane, but there are times when I am still ashamed to use it. I don't like to use it in front of friends or loved ones who are ignorant of, or uncomfortable with, my vision loss. I fear running into people who have only known me as a fully sighted person and having to explain myself. There are times when I despise my cane. Sometimes I want to throw it away so I can walk through a crowd unnoticed like everyone else. But I cannot. The whole point of a white cane is to be noticed.

****

There are times when I think partial, deteriorating vision is even harder to live with than total blindness. "Get it over with once and for all," I sometimes say to myself. My poor vision necessitates constant readjusting of my life, and I feel as though I experience a little taste of death almost every day. For example, I recently discovered that I can no longer read subtitles in foreign movies. Not long ago I opened a favorite novel and found that I had to use a magnifying glass to read it. That never used to happen. I need to make the text on my computer screen larger and larger when I write. I can no longer see stars, boats on the horizon, or the face of a lover in the dark.

Vision should not be thought of in terms of absolutes. The fact that someone doesn't use a white cane does not necessarily mean he or she is fully sighted. By the same token, the presence of a cane does not always suggest total blindness. The fact that I do have vision, even though it is very poor, causes a great deal of confusion among those around me. People are taken aback when they try to help me across the street and I look them in the eye and tell them I do not need assistance. I have even been accused of pretending to be blind. What I would like is the understanding that the cane means I need a bit of extra help to see, not that I am unable to see anything at all. I walk with a cane, but I also wear a watch and carry a newspaper.

I am one of the sighted blind.

A LONG JOURNEY HOME

by Carol A. Howe

For the first several years of my life I did not know that there was anything wrong with me. I had attended kindergarten at the local public school along with all the other neighborhood children, but then at the beginning of the first grade I found myself being bussed to an unfamiliar building.

This new school, it turned out, had a special program to accommodate children with vision problems. I recall being in a classroom with regular students, but I felt like an outsider. My schoolbooks had the same titles as those of my classmates, but my books were bigger in size and written in large print. I hated this new place and fought it every step of the way because I did not want to be singled out as "different." I wanted to be just like all the other kids.

Within a month or two, I returned to the school where I had attended kindergarten. At first, a woman from the special school would periodically visit me after class, bringing me those dreaded large-print books. I still vaguely remember talking with this woman at the back of the classroom. She had dark brown hair and wore a dark-colored dress. I wanted no part of her visits or of this special treatment, and after letting my parents know this, they honored my request. I imagine the woman may have been relieved—as a young child, my anger and frustration were not very well concealed.

I was born with a less-than-normal amount of pigment in my eyes. For me, this congenital eye condition manifests in weak central vision and an involuntary jittery movement of the eyes called nystagmus. I also had astigmatism in each eye, which blurred the edges of what I did see. At age three, my eyesight was measured at 20/200. My visual acuity has actually improved somewhat as I've grown older, and the involuntary movement of my eyes is barely perceptible now unless I am tired or concentrating especially hard. This side-to-side movement was quite noticeable when I was a child, however, and it made me the target of ruthless teasing.

One of my clearest and most painful memories of childhood is the day a schoolmate ran over to me, looked me straight in the face, and burst out laughing. She called out to another kid, "Boy, you were right!" suggesting that my eyes—and I—had been a topic of derisive discussion amongst these children just moments before. The girl's menacing smirk and mocking laughter are forever engraved in my mind.

From my point of view as a child, being different from others was the absolute worst. To me, being different—I would now say unique—had nothing but negative, hurtful connotations. I have had to learn the hard way that adults can be every bit as insensitive and cruel as can children. As an adult, however, I have gained a broader perspective. I now realize that being unique can be a wonderful and liberating thing. It took me many years, though, before I could truly feel there was anything at all wonderful about my uniqueness.

I believe my parents did the best they could with a difficult situation. But they were caught up in the dynamics of their own difficult relationship, which adversely affected my growing sense of anger, frustration and isolation. On some level, I felt my condition was at least partly responsible for their unhappiness.

School was not a particularly enjoyable experience for me. I was always terrified of being singled out and taunted. It was nearly impossible for me to speak up and tell the teacher that I needed to sit in the front row in order to see, or that I could not read something on the blackboard. At some point, unbeknownst to me, my parents contacted my school and requested that it be subtly arranged for me to be seated up in front. Even if I sat as close to the chalkboard as possible, though, there were times when I still could not decipher what was written on it. I usually kept quiet, though. The last thing I wanted to do was to draw attention to myself.

Glasses helped the astigmatism somewhat, but I rarely wore them. Since glasses did little to improve my distance vision, I still needed to get really close in order to see many things, and I was terrified that this would make me the target of unwanted scrutiny and teasing among my schoolmates. So, instead of using my glasses to help me see, I would usually wear them on top of my head (as if that went unnoticed).

Early childhood photographs of me suggest that I was a happy little girl who loved to have fun. Repeated verbal attacks by other kids, however, were taking their toll, and at a young age, I began retreating into a safe inner world. I had subconsciously concluded that the easiest way to handle painful situations was to remove myself from them, both emotionally and physically. I had a few playmates in the neighborhood who I felt accepted me, but I was not eager to be thrust into new and unfamiliar situations in which I might not be able to handle something because of my low vision, or where new kids might pick on me. My escapes were my colorful inner fantasies, a few close and trusted friends, television, and listening to music.

I felt unprepared to cope with the world, particularly with other people. I was confused, and in retrospect, I'm not sure that I quite understood what was going on, or why kids were teasing me. Somehow I had missed out on learning how to get along with others or how to form healthy relationships. My low vision may well have been a factor in preventing me from clearly observing how other kids did things, which in turn prevented me from readily fitting in, or from grasping things that were visually obvious to most people.

From my defensive stance, I saw the world as an adversary, and I was constantly on guard. Needless to say, my beliefs about the world and myself, although perhaps understandable, were self-defeating, and they negatively affected all facets of my life, particularly my relationships with other people. Anger, frustration, and confusion created a great deal of hostility, which in turn distanced me from people all the more.

I grew up with a sense of being deficient, of missing some essential "piece" that everyone possessed but me. I felt somehow "less" than other people, and I felt I had to work much harder than others to be accepted and loved. I grew to resent this, and I became very self-rejecting and unforgiving of my perceived deficit.

I did have a keen sense of hearing, which is probably true of most visually impaired people. I also possessed excellent peripheral vision, and, as I mentioned previously, my visual acuity improved somewhat with the passing years. After many struggles I managed to obtain a driver's license at age seventeen. I had lived in the same city since I was three years old, and my familiarity with the local streets, along with an excellent memory for detail, greatly facilitated my driving expertise. To my knowledge, I was my opthalmologist's only patient with similar visual limitations who received a driver's license. As it happens, I have not driven in several years, but this is primarily because I relocated to a city where public transportation is good and parking is horrendous.

As a teenager and in my twenties, I spent most of my time safely locked away in my head, removed from the pain I believed I would suffer if I allowed myself to get too close to the external world. In later years I came to realize what a scary place one's mind can truly be, but this inner refuge felt safe as a younger person, even with the relentless barrage of self-recriminations and self-rejecting thoughts. I was accustomed to feeling an ongoing sense of defeat and unhappiness; at least it was familiar, and I knew that I could handle it. I was also growing weary of trying to pretend I had normal vision, and maintaining a comfortable distance from the world gave me relief from this stress as well.

In my early thirties, hoping to change this pattern of behavior, I sought therapy. My primary goal was to improve my relationships with other people, particularly with men. My therapist introduced me to several new and positive ways of relating to myself and the world around me, based on a more spiritual approach to life, and I became gradually aware of a deep inner journey upon which I was embarking.

The process of self-discovery that ensued was exhilarating to me. I eagerly delved into an examination of my childhood, and I began to understand more fully the old beliefs I had developed as a response to painful childhood experiences. I labored mightily to replace these old ways of thinking with healthier beliefs that would better serve me in engaging the world. In retrospect, I think my perfectionist tendencies were also pushing me to work hard at this process. If I could achieve the unattainable goal of perfection, then perhaps I could compensate for my vision deficit as well.

I am determined to keep forging ahead on this path of discovery and transformation. I have lately managed to create a much more loving, joyful, and supportive relationship with myself, and this has had a positive impact on my relationship with other people. I now appreciate the fact that being different from others can actually be very rewarding, and for the first time I truly enjoy the fact that I am unique. My distance vision may be limited and a bit blurry, but my intuitive perception of people and situations is often crystal-clear.

During this process of soul-searching, I have uncovered deep conflicts between the person I would truly like to be and the person I became due to my eye condition. I spent most of my life retreating from social situations, and also, I now realize, from love, which is utterly contrary to my true nature. No more! I have found that I am basically a very social and outgoing person. I thrive on newness and diversity, yet in the past I was often paralyzed with fear over confronting new people and situations.

Coping mechanisms that I developed long ago to live with my poor vision directly relate to key talents that I now utilize daily in my career as a computer systems analyst. Examples of these talents include: Creative problem-solving and in-depth analysis (using my intellect to figure things out); my tendency to be thorough and detail-oriented (partly due to the fear that I will miss something pertinent because I cannot see it); the fact that I am well-organized (I use placement—the knowledge and memory of where items are located and in what order—so that I do not need to rely solely on my vision to locate things). My career is very visual in that I work at a computer much of the time, and I thrive on autonomy and self-expression.

Living with low vision has absolutely strengthened me as a person. The fact that I was forced to develop coping strategies in order to meet everyday visual obstacles has bred a deep sense of accomplishment and creative success. It is amazing how inventive one becomes in order to overcome the obstacles of a physical limitation and maintain a strong sense of independence. I developed powerful determination and resilience in my desire to live a normal life. This determination gave me the strength to persevere in my journey of personal and spiritual discovery, even though the process became unbearably painful and confusing at times.

Would my life be different had I not been born with a congenital eye problem? Undoubtedly! But it may not have been nearly as satisfying. I now appreciate how lucky I truly am. I have assumed the responsibility for creating the kind of life experiences that I desire, and my energies are focused on making these things happen.

Had my life unfolded in any other way, I might not feel the profound joy and deep contentment that characterizes my life today. I can say without hesitation that the greatest moments of my life—the most intense feelings of fulfillment and contentment that I have ever felt—have come about as a result of a conscious inner journey. My experiences surrounding my poor vision led me to focus more internally and gave me the determination to learn about myself and come to terms with the events of my life. Telling my story to you here only brings me one step closer to complete and liberating self-acceptance.

MOXIE

by Kelly Weiss

I was born two months premature, which meant I had to be in an incubator for eight weeks. Everything was fine until the oxygen level accidentally went from 40% to 80%. What happened as a result is called retrolental fibroplasia. The excess oxygen basically burned the retinas of my eyes.

After six months, my parents couldn't understand why I was unable to focus. They went to several different doctors and finally found one who told them I was blind and why. It was hard for my mom and dad when they found out, especially my mom. But over time she has coped with it just fine.

When I was two, I began attending the Blind Children's Center. It was an ordinary nursery school, except it was for blind children. While I was there I learned about everyday struggles and what it's like to be a kid. I learned how to drink milk properly, eat with a spoon, play with other kids, play with toys, share, and so on. My family also had to learn from my teachers that being blind was not a bad thing; it can be a wonderful thing. Even though it was hard, life was good because I was still going to be able to walk and talk and play with other kids like everyone else.

I lived at the school Monday through Thursday and would come home on weekends. My family loved the idea that I would be home every weekend. The situation wasn't easy for my sister, Tracy, but she tried very hard. She played with me every day I was home. We would play tag and hide-and-seek together—all those games. I would ride tricycles and run around in the backyard with her. That was a lot of fun for me.

I went to the Blind Children's Center until I was about

seven. After that I went to a regular public school in Santa Monica—a mainstream school with sighted kids. I was with four other blind children in a resource program where we learned to read and write in Braille, add and subtract, and do all the different things sighted kids do. At nine-and-a-half I was able to go into a classroom where I was the only blind student. My teacher tried very hard to get me involved with the other kids. She treated me like the rest of the students and didn't put up with any garbage. Whenever I tried to pull something or get out of doing work, she would call me on it and encourage me to do more.

My mobility instructor taught me how to use a cane that year. We would go walking in residential areas and cross at stoplights. Stoplights were hard for me, but once I understood the distinction between perpendicular and parallel traffic, I was fine. It was fun being able to travel by myself. I went from doing it with assistance to having my teacher follow me in a car. My resource teacher was always encouraging me, telling me I could do anything I wanted as long as I put my mind to it. He was the best teacher I could have had, and he's partly why I am doing so well today.

When I was thirteen, I entered junior high school. Those were three hard years. I was the only blind student in the school, and lots of kids made fun of me. They didn't know how to handle my blindness. But I also made some wonderful friends who understood that being blind doesn't mean anything is wrong with me. It just means I have one little nuisance; my eyes don't work, and I have to learn how to adjust.

If I had to write a history report or a book report, I would do it in Braille. Then, because the teachers didn't know how to read Braille, I would have to type it for them. God forbid I should take my mind off typing for an instant. Total concentration was the name of the game. I might think I was typing okay, but if I didn't concentrate I would make a lot of mistakes.

My teachers were thrilled that I was typing my assignments; in fact, they felt typed work was even better than handwritten. They were pleased a student like me wanted to type my reports. But I'll tell you, doing homework was hard. If the rest of the students had two hours of homework, I had four because of the brailling and typing. You can imagine how that made me feel sometimes. But it was okay, because in high school I started playing the violin in the student orchestra, and I always had that to look forward to. That always helped me relieve the stress.

In high school I joined a group called Young Life. We would meet at a different person's house once a week, and the whole purpose was to help you make friends. I was the only blind person there. We did skits and sang songs about the Lord. They also wanted me to go to their camp in the country. I was able to go there when I was eighteen because they had someone acting as my guide.

There were some unusual things about the camp, like the zip line, where I was strapped into a harness and then slid seven hundred feet down a rope and into the lake. It didn't scare me. It never even occurred to me that I might run into a tree, that the rope might break, or that I might get hurt. Twice in one day I jumped off the deck and into the lake. One of the campers said, "You're insane. I'd never do that if I was blind. I'd be too afraid." But I had no fear at all. I also walked a tightrope and went horseback riding. I got a bravery award at the end for doing all those fabulous things.

That same year I joined another group called Project Interdependence, which had people with and without disabilities. The purpose of the group was to accept people for who they were and not say things like "she's blind" or "he's crippled." We were taught to say that a person was visually challenged or visually impaired, or that they used a wheelchair or crutches. That way we weren't putting labels on people.

At that camp we had to jump fifty feet into the air in a harness, with no rope to hold on to; we just had to trust our bodies. I was a little bit scared, but once I jumped off, I never worried that I might hurt myself. It was great. People couldn't believe that a blind person could do such a thing.

One time all the kids had to put blindfolds on their faces to see what it would be like to be visually impaired. I agreed to be in a wheelchair for one hour instead, and I insisted they tie my legs together so I would know what it felt like to be paralyzed. We also had to stand on tables and fall into the hands of a trusted person. We never got hurt.

My graduation from high school was a terrific experience that I will never forget. It was wonderful being able to graduate with the class like everyone else. The only thing I couldn't do was play in the orchestra while we marched, but that didn't bother me; I just wanted to get out. I'd had enough of school.

My mom gave me quite a graduation present. She took me to England, where she was born, so I could meet my cousins. It was a great cultural experience, and I feel culture is important. We went to London and visited Westminster Abbey, where I was allowed to touch everything. One of my favorite things was the praying statue with its hands crossed. We also went all over Wales; I liked walking on the rocks at Agmwar-by-the-Sea.

After high school I attended Santa Monica College, where I took several computer courses, and in 1988 I went to the Living Skills Independent Center in Northern California. That's where I learned a lot about myself. The main question I had to answer was: "Can I take care of myself should anything happen to my family?" (The answer was yes.) I had already learned how to do some cooking and cleaning from a private tutor when I was fifteen, but at the Center I learned how to sweep and mop, which I hadn't learned before. I also learned how to write checks, which is something I'd really wanted to learn. I stayed at the Center for nine months, then I came home and took a couple of months off to re-orient myself, and to use the skills I had learned up north. My mom couldn't believe what a changed person I was. She hardly had to do anything for me, and she still doesn't because I won't let her.

That fall I got a part-time job answering phones for the Unified School District and went back to Santa Monica College. I took English classes, transcription, and computer classes. In addition, I went to an occupational center for about three years, where I learned medical terminology and transcription. I had a great medical teacher there. She treated me like an equal and didn't simply accept it when I made mistakes.

In 1994 I received my certificate, and a job developer got me acquainted with the Veteran's Administration Hospital. I got a job at the hospital as a medical transcriber in the radiology department, which is where I am now. My goal, however, is to become a motivational speaker ten or fifteen years down the line, because transcription is not all that I can do. I recently took an oral communication course to learn more about myself and others and to learn how to be more outgoing, self-confident and secure. I know I can do more, and do better.

This year, after five years of hard work, I completed the L.A. Marathon. The marathon is a big event, with close to forty thousand people participating. There were people passing out water and candy and orange slices, telling me, "Mile fifteen; you're almost there. Eleven miles and you'll be there." The cheering and music at the event were incredible!

I walked the course instead of running, but I was still sore the next day because walking eight hours and thirty minutes like that takes a lot out of you. But I'll tell you, it really taught me something about myself. I can do a lot more than a lot of people think I can, or even I think I can. I'll definitely do another marathon. Maybe I'll even decide I want to run it.

Whatever it is you want to do, I'd just like to say, "Go for it." Don't limit yourself. It will expand your life and enhance the way you think about yourself and the way others think about you. At work, at school, wherever you are, my advice is to keep on trying and welcoming new experiences. It works.

LOOKING TO THE LEFT

by Henry Pasa

In June 1985 I was working for a California bank during a very stressful time; we were acquiring another bank. It was during this period that I started suffering from very severe headaches. I am told I was popping aspirin continuously during the day in an effort to stave off the pain. On the evening of June 5, after a full day of work, I returned home, again with a severe headache. During the night I collapsed. It turned out that what I had been suffering from was not a stress headache but a cerebral hemorrhage.

The following day, when I failed to show up for work, two members of my department came looking for me. They found me on the floor of my bedroom in a state of semi-consciousness—the result of a burst aneurysm in my brain. I was taken to San Francisco General Hospital, where I underwent an emergency craniotomy. When I came out of the coma, I found myself with extensive retrograde amnesia, as well as an inability to remember events that were presently occurring in my life.

I was unaware until then that I also had a problem with my eyes, known as an hemonymous hemianopsia, which blocked my left field of vision. For example, if I looked at a clock—let's say it was 2:45—I would see the little hand between the two and three, but I would not see the big hand, so it would not make any sense to me. It made me effectively unable to tell time.

That was thirteen years ago, and I have had to master many coping mechanisms during the intervening years. I have learned, for example, that when I look at anything, I must always scan from left to right, focusing carefully on the left portion of my visual field. One of the most maddening difficulties I have is a tendency to clip off prefixes or short words when I read. I was recently reading a book by a professor who had gone blind, in which she wrote the following sentence: "I kept delaying paying my bills because I was a miser or didn't have the money."

I continued reading, but then I thought, "Wait a minute..." I went back to reread the aformentioned sentence, and upon closer scrutiny, I discovered it was actually written as follows: "I kept delaying paying my bills, not because I was a miser or didn't have the money." Because my hermianopsia makes me liable to miss short words, I had missed the word "not," which changed the meaning of the sentence entirely.

If I'm reading a magazine or a dime-store novel I allow myself to read quickly, because if I clip off a prefix, it's no big deal. But if I'm reading something that deals with, say, assembling a product at home—putting together a new appliance or hooking up a television, for example—then I have to read very carefully in order to make sure I don't clip off a prefix or a negative in front of a word, which of course would foul up the whole procedure.

When I'm in a public place, I've learned to scan as far left as possible before I start reading. This helps avoid the confusion and embarrassment that would often ensue due to missing words or phrases when reading. One example of this used to occur with some regularity. While looking for the men's restroom, I would see a door marked M-E-N and start to enter, only to find myself in a room full of women. I had, of course, failed to see the letters W-O preceeding M-E-N.

I have also learned that when speaking with someone, I should always make eye contact with their right eye. That way their entire face is in my field of vision. This is important to me because a lot of communication is achieved through facial expression, and I prefer to see people's expressions when I'm talking to them. The only people with whom I don't feel I need to make this effort are close friends I'm extremely comfortable around.

At some point after my injury, when I realized my vision loss would be permanent, I made up my mind to give up driving. I still had a valid driver's license when I visited my best friend in Georgia, however, and he allowed me to drive his car on a country road. That proved to be an interesting experience, to say the least.

I found myself focusing on the hemianopic—the blind spot on the left side of my field of vision—to the point of ignoring what was on my right, sighted side. As a result, the car was always drifting off to the right. My friend had to holler at me several times, "Henry, you're going off the road!" And sure enough, I was veering off to the right. Of course, I was completely unaware that I was doing this, so it seems my decision to give up driving was a good one. Can you imagine me trying to drive in a city?

Another problem that arises frequently is that when I walk down the street people have a tendency to cut in front of me. This is perfectly normal; I'm sure everybody does it—I'm sure I used to do it. But now with my blind spot, when somebody is cutting in from my left—and especially if they're moving quickly—I'm not aware of them until they're right in front of me and I bang right into them. Now I try to scan carefully when I walk down the street, but I can't always do this, particularly in a crowded area. No matter how hard I try, I often can't scan fast enough since so many people are moving about me so quickly. It's like watching a movie and missing all the action on the left side of the screen because I'm not scanning quickly enough. But I've learned to accommodate the disability as best I can. It's something I can live with.

MY STORY

by Britt Lincoln

I was born in Akron, Ohio, on September 15, 1978. I had no nose, mouth, or eyes, and my eye sockets were twice as far apart as they should have been. In spite of all these problems, though, my parents were determined to give me as normal a life as possible.

My life was far from normal for the first few years, however. An ear problem threatened my hearing when I was less than three months old that necessitated the implantation of a set of plastic tubes. These tubes drained the fluid that was collecting in my ear canals and causing my near-total deafness. They ended up needing to be replaced three times, the final time with a set of steel tubes rather than the plastic ones I'd had previously. I was treated by four eye doctors before one was finally found who could make suitable plastic eyes for me. Several reconstructive surgeries on my face were also performed during this time.

As if all these medical problems weren't enough to contend with, my parents decided to move to eastern Kentucky when I was two-and-a-half years old. This move affected not only my education, but also my relationship with an extraordinarily warm-hearted hospital volunteer who had become my godmother. When I lived in Ohio I could see my godmother daily if I wanted because her house was just minutes away from ours. The move to Kentucky put us seven hours apart, so my trips to visit her were cut to one per year.

Another reason I didn't like this change of scene was because I had to get used to a new house and yard. For months I kept telling my parents that I wanted to go home, not fully understanding that Kentucky was my home.

Eventually, though, I caught on and stopped asking to go home all the time, and my parents started to think about my education.

If we had stayed in Ohio, I would have had access to an excellent school with a highly qualified vision teacher. Neither of these resources existed in eastern Kentucky. To prepare me for school, my mother, father, and occasionally my godmother would read books to me. My books were printed in a format known as twin-vision, allowing me to discover Braille by feeling the embossed characters while a sighted person read the corresponding print. In this way I was introduced to the world of literacy.

The social aspects of preparing for school were not so easily addressed. The series of operations I'd undergone had made me severly autistic. For those unfamiliar with autism, it is a condition whose chief symptom is the inability to tolerate sensory stimulation. On top of this, I was extremely shy. To ease me out of my autism, my mother found a pre-school run by the local university, which I attended more frequently as time went on. This pre-school did wonders for me, and I began to lose both my shyness and my fear of being touched. By age five I was ready to enter kindergarten.

I completed kindergarten through the fifth grade at a small school with an extremely open-minded group of teachers. At first, school was a major struggle. Braille seemed impossibly difficult to learn, and I did not know any of my new classmates. This turbulent period lasted only a few months, though. A multitude of classroom activities and an unusually skilled kindergarten teacher eventually helped me make friends.

My problems with Braille were solved by degrees. My vision teacher was very impatient and would raise her voice at me all the time, but as I became more proficient she gradually stopped yelling so much. It was during kindergarten that I decided to someday become a vision teacher and teach Braille the way I thought it should be taught; that is, with patience and praise rather than with drill sergeant tactics.

The rest of my elementary school years were relatively easy. I learned that if I needed further explanation of a concept I could ask for it without fear of ridicule. If I knew the answer to a question, I could raise my hand and be reasonably sure the teacher would call on me. I was not given special treatment academically, but I was not downgraded, either. In fact, I was encouraged to take an active part in my own education by participating in yearly "individual education plan" meetings.

Physically navigating around the school building soon became as trouble-free as dealing with the teachers. Initially, I got around by trailing the walls, but gradually I mastered the techniques of cane travel. My social life was also improving, which helped a great deal. By the middle of the second grade I had become best friends with a girl named Janie, a low-income student with a heart of gold. When I got a little older I often had sleepovers with her. I had other good friends, too, but none quite as kind and supportive as Janie.

Several more facial surgeries occurred during my elementary school years, but the resulting periods of homebound instruction did not set me back academically or socially. School work could be done just as easily at home as at school, and even though I didn't have daily contact with my friends, they didn't forget about me during my long absences. Friends were pretty much inaccessible during my recoveries from surgery, but the medical professionals I saw were very responsive to my needs. Negotiating with them about my care supplemented the advocacy training I received from the individual education plan meetings, and Britt Lincoln the self-advocate began to emerge.

Surgeries took a back seat to family problems at the beginning of the fifth grade when my father decided to leave my mother. I could not understand why he would choose another woman over his wife, and it was difficult for me when he moved out. I responded by strengthening my relationships with several old friends, who—along with my therapists—helped me accept my father's abandonment of our family.

Middle school posed a whole new set of challenges for me. The school served students from five area elementary schools in addition to my own, and the building itself was much larger than my previous school. I was effectively separated from Janie when she and I were assigned to different homerooms; in middle school, if you were not in the same homeroom you did not attend the same classes, either. A mobility teacher taught me the basic layout of the school, and other instructors came to my rescue when I would occasionally get lost on my way to classes.

The idea of moving to a new classroom every hour was a new one to me. At my old school we stayed in one room all day, except for lunch and recess. It wasn't hard to get used to the new system, though, because it was actually kind of fun to get up and move every hour. The separation from Janie was more difficult for me to come to terms with. Several discussions with the guidance counselor and the principal failed to get us assigned to the same homeroom, so I made do with seeing her at lunch and on the bus.

I tried not to be overly concerned about seeing my best friend all the time, and I made a lot of other friends to try and fill the void. With the aid of a special teacher for the learning disabled, and later a teacher of the visually impaired, I started refining my assertiveness skills. The work load in middle school was much heavier than it had been in elementary school, and I was advised that it was no crime to ask for a reduction in a long math assignment or an extension on a big science project since it took a lot more time for me to do certain things than it did sighted students.

This was a revelation to me because I thought being a normal student meant doing the same work in the same amount of time as other students, without exception. Sometimes it was tempting for me to abuse these requests for special privileges, but I soon learned not to do this. On the whole, I feel I did a good job of overcoming the various social and academic challenges I faced in middle school. It did not make matters any easier, though, when I had to undergo a final series of operations, bringing the total number of surgeries in my lifetime to twenty-two. It had been a long journey.

These years were not all toil and no fun, however. During the summers my mother allowed me to spend time with my godmother back in Ohio and my grandmother in Pennsylvania. I rarely got to see either of them during the school year, so spending time alone with them was a real treat. They exposed me to nature, museums, and too many other things to list here. My mother also took me with her on trips to North Carolina, Virginia, Texas, Washington State and Washington, D.C., to attend conferences, consult medical professionals, and visit friends and relatives. Traveling to other states and going to conferences for my mother's job broadened my horizons quite a bit, but they were about to get even broader.

For the first three years of high school I attended the Kentucky School for the Blind (KSB), a boarding school. Through a special program I was also able to spend part of each day at a nearby public school. It was during this time that I discovered how much my social skills had been neglected. If a teacher gave an assignment I wasn't sure I could do, I would cry openly in class. I also found that I had trouble interacting with people my own age. One of the reasons was that I had always been encouraged to use big words in everyday conversation, but the kids in my class considered big words totally uncool. They had their own version of the English language, and it wasn't the same as mine.

With coaching from a wonderful vision teacher and several caring adult friends, I became more patient and more determined. Mastering the lingo of teenagers took time, but eventually I was able to use their words and phrases in a reasonably natural manner. This opened the door to my interactions with peers.

Other ways in which I tried to improve my social skills were by participating in track, forensics, and chorus, which enabled me to meet people from other states, which I found quite exciting. My extracurricular activities also taught me that even if I was not fully successful at a given venture—track, in my case—I could still benefit from the experience by making friends with teammates and discovering new ways to deal with stress without complaining. This valuable lesson would serve me well later on.

For my sophmore and junior years I was placed in a program in which the students did housekeeping chores such as cooking and cleaning. We were also responsible for reporting any problems to maintenance without the supervision of a cottage parent. I feel the program was only moderately successful for me. I became proficient at a number of cleaning tasks, but I was never really able to cook a meal on my own.

When I became a senior I decided to leave KSB and finish high school in my home county. I chose to do this in large part because I had trouble with certain of the teaching practices at KSB. Teachers and administrators there appeared willing to negotiate with students when disagreements arose, but that willingness was only skin deep. I felt the teachers at my local school would be more receptive to my needs and more willing to make compromises, so I made the transfer over the strenuous objections of my parents.

My parents' objections stemmed mainly from the fact that our county in Kentucky had no resources for visually impaired students, but concerns over that issue were dealt with when the county hired a vision teacher. The year was a monster academically because I took pre-calculus and chemistry, but I didn't hesitate to stick up for myself in order to get the visual aides and tutoring I needed. Once in a while I had to border on being rude to get the things I required, but this was a last resort.

My senior year was a breakthrough for me socially,

thanks to a freshman named Derek. He became my boyfriend the first week of the school year. I went to the Valentine's Day Dance and the prom with him, and my mother never had to worry about us because he was too young to drive.

Toward the end of my senior year everyone got a vicious case of graduation fever. I was very happy I had returned to my hometown to finish high school. I thought it only proper to graduate with my childhood friends. Many of my classmates were planning to attend Morehead State, the local university, but I had already been offered admission to the University of Kentucky.

After a flurry of parties and some preparatory training at a rehabilitation center, I enrolled at UK. The bus system there proved to be a life-saver for me because even though my cane-travel skills are pretty good, my street-crossing abilities aren't the greatest. The bus drivers have all gotten to know me, and they always treat me with genuine courtesy. A cell phone has also come in handy; if I have an emergency when I'm away from my apartment, I can easily get it dealt with.

Occasional emergencies have actually helped me discover that there is a middle ground between non-confrontational assertiveness and rudeness. Until I entered college I thought the only way to be assertive was to keep my voice calm and politely state what it was I needed. Several of the administrators at UK have helped me realize that sometimes civil, rational discourse is not enough to get urgent problems solved.

For example, one year I made arrangements to go to a major convention of the National Federation of the Blind, but at the last minute one of my teachers refused to excuse me from class in order to attend. She felt the convention did not merit an excused absence. I spoke to an administrator to stress that being with other blind people at the convention was a valuable opportunity for me. This approach worked, and I was granted an excused absence to attend the convention.

Most of my professors have been extremely responsive to my needs. When I need to utilize their office hours but don't know how to get to their offices, they agree to meet me in a familiar place and work with me there. Extensions on assignments are also easy to arrange when I need them, but I try to ask for them as little as possible. I try my best to do the same work in the same amount of time as other UK students.

I belong to a Christian Student Fellowship and the Sigma Kappa sorority, both of which are full of friendly people who have given me support and guidance. In spite of the academic and logistical hurdles and the ups and downs of social life, I love college. I have become an education major, and after I finish my bachelor's degree, I plan to get a master's degree in teaching the visually impaired. I feel I have a rich social life as well as a promising academic one. I look forward to applying the lessons I have learned in the teaching profession.

BREAKING THE BARRIERS OF BLINDNESS

by Elena Storer Lass

Finding pathways of learning and living beyond vision is a challenge. Taking an overview of my life, I realize that my widowed mother was forever finding ways to provide opportunities for her two little girls. School, music lessons, church, the local girls' club, summer camp, and college were all ways in which she encouraged us to broaden our horizons. We made friends every step of the way.

My first encounter with blind people was as a high school student in Oakland. A group of vision-impaired students from the California School for the Deaf and Blind were mainstreamed there, and I became a reader for one of these students, Leora. Subsequently, she and I enrolled at Mills College in Oakland, where I continued to be one of her readers; we graduated together in 1931. Leora pursued a career in social service, and over the years we continued to enjoy a special friendship, meeting at class reunions and visiting on the telephone.

In spite of her blindness, Leora was dauntless in her pursuit of justice, including cases in which she was profesionally involved. In her personal life she enjoyed a wonderful and caring romance, which was sadly cut short by the early death of her companion, David. After this loss, however, she remained steadfast in her commitment to David's sister Ethel, who suffered from a terminal illness. Leora became her legal guardian, assuming full responsibility for Ethel's medical, legal, and social needs. I learned a great deal from Leora.

****

After graduating from college I went on to earn certification in Special Education from U.C. Berkeley, and I worked for a time as a speech therapist in the local school district, where I frequently had students with limited vision and/or hearing. A memorable opportunity to observe other blind caregivers occurred when my husband, Lowell, and I traveled to Afghanistan in 1966. Our traveling companion was a preacher who also happened to be the editor of the Oakland Tribune. Two missionaries, Dr. Wilson and his wife, Priscilla, were working in Afghanistan with the Presbyterian Church at the time of our visit.

Dr. Wilson had noticed that many people in Kabul had vision problems. As part of their involvement with the community, the Wilsons invited a handful of local people to come to their home for craft sessions. These sessions became so popular that the Wilsons ultimately formed a school on the grounds of their compound for blind residents of Kabul. Here they received instruction not only in crafts, but also in English, basic hygiene and bible study.

The Wilsons were curious as to why so many people in Kabul were blind. On a hunch, Dr. Wilson took samples from the local drinking water source and brought the samples back to San Francisco for testing. The tests revealed the source of an infection known to cause blindness, and Dr. Wilson returned to Afghanistan with a cure—fertile duck eggs—which he carried in a box on his lap. When the eggs hatched, the young ducks were set out on the water to feed, and they ate the larvae that caused the infection. In gratitude for his contribution to community health, Dr. Wilson received distinguished recognition from the government in Kabul.

****

I feel I have always been able to find new opportunities in my own life, in spite of the often formidable obstacles. I believe these ups and downs have prepared me to accept the reality that I myself am now going blind, and to face the fact that macular degeneration of the retina cannot be reversed.

I now live in a large senior housing community. I am no longer able to read print, but I feel the opportunities available to us are almost endless. There are concerts, seminars, athletics, and various clubs one can join depending on one's interests. A local organization, Beyond Eyes, hosts a monthly Sunday afternoon mixer for over one hundred people, which I try to attend. (Editor's note: Elena is the facilitator and the major mover and shaker of Beyond Eyes.) I truly feel there is no dearth of opportunities for those who choose to seek them.

In staying positive and leading a healthy life without vision, I cannot overstate the value of friendships—listening to one another, sharing ideas, and volunteering for small, manageable tasks. Without question, losing my eyesight has been a big nuisance, but it has not limited my involvement in the life of my family, my church or my community. The full acceptance of my condition may only come with time, but the determination to persevere rests entirely with me. I wouldn't have it any other way.

I SEE, JUST IN A DIFFERENT WAY

by Richard King

An important beginning in my life occured in 1978. It was something that might be considered more of an ending by many people, but I do not see it that way. I am referring to the onset of the disease that ultimately caused my visual impairment.

When I was eight years old and in the third grade my teacher noticed that I was reading with my book held closer to my face than the other children. When she asked me to try reading with the book a normal distance away, we discovered that I could not see well enough to read. She phoned my mother to advise her about the situation, and my mom picked me up from school and took me to the optometrist that afternoon. After examining me, the optometrist told us he wasn't sure why, but I had lost a major portion of the vision in my left eye and that something was wrong with my right eye as well. He advised us to go to an opthalmologist for further diagnosis.

Over the next year we went from doctor to doctor, and I went in and out of the hospital four times. We did, however, finally get a diagnosis at the end of it all. My neuroopthalmologist told us that I had a hereditary condition called Lieber's optic atrophy. He said the disease was very rare, and he told us that even though my mom has normal vision, she was a carrier for the disease. He explained that the disease usually strikes people between twenty-five and forty years of age. The early onset in my case is a large part of why it had taken so long to diagnose me.

The doctor told us that the condition was stabilized. This suggests that it is unlikely my vision will diminish any further. The disease attacks the optic nerve so the impairment is perceptual in nature. Essentially, this means that even though my eyes can technically see things the same way everyone else does, I am not getting the message to the visual center of my brain the same way. This impairment affects my vision in both eyes, but not equally; I see better out of my right eye than out of my left. Also, I see better peripherally than I do centrally. For this reason I cannot read print, but I can negotiate my way through most environments fairly easily.

One of the first major challenges I faced was in reading. We knew about Braille because my mom's sister and her mother both have similar conditions. For my part, I had to set about the process of changing schools and getting into a class where I could learn Braille. I hated it at first, and at times I felt angry and frustrated. However, one of the things that kept me going throughout the whole process was my mom. She learned Braille at the same time I did, and she refused to let me give up. When I would start to feel sorry for myself, she would let me know that she had no desire to come to my pity party.

The struggle we went through at that time was as much about accepting my situation as it was about learning Braille. My mom made it clear to me every step of the way that just because learning Braille was hard didn't mean I was excused from working at it. So even though it was difficult for me, I learned Braille with a lot of help and a lot of pushing. This was a pivotal point in what I call my cycle of acceptance. Overcoming the barrier that print posed to my reading ability invalidated the "I can't" excuse and at the same time restored my access to education.

I transfered to a school that had a special program for kids with visual impairments. The school also had a mainstreaming program, and I was fully mainstreamed; that is, I was in a class with regular students. I did all the same work and learned all the same things as they did. The only difference was that my materials were in Braille and on tape. This was a great experience because it taught me that although I was doing things a bit differently, I could still do all the things other students did.

Overall, I liked being mainstreamed very much. I knew I was getting the same education as everyone else, and it gave me a chance to interact with peers who were sighted as well as those who were blind. However, mainstreaming was hard at times because of the obstacles that people tried to put in front of me. For instance, my placement in a particular class was not always immediately accepted. In fact, in two separate instances I remember it being challenged.

The first time this happened was at the start of the fifth grade. The teacher felt she needed extra time to set up the classroom and find a reader for me before I could come into the class. After a few days my parents made it clear that even if a reader was not yet available, the teacher needed to make a place for me in the class. She did, and that was the end of the conflict from my perspective. By the end of that school year she had become one of my biggest advocates.

The second time something like this happened was near the end of my sophomore year of high school. It was time to choose classes for the following year, and I wanted to take the advanced placement biology class. The problem was that although I had the grades and all the prerequisites, the teacher would not admit me. She felt my presence in the class would be a lot of extra work for her, and she also felt I would not do well on the advanced placement exam. Her argument was essentially that I would be taking a spot that would be better utilized by a sighted student.

My parents threatened legal action, and the school district decided to take the decision out of the biology teacher's hands. She was ordered to enroll me in her class, and as things turned out I got an A for the semester and scored high marks on the national exam. In fact, I developed such a good relationship with this teacher over the course of the school year that she ended up writing me a letter of recommendation for college.

I don't mean to suggest that I have successfully broken through all the barriers of my visual impairment and emerged unscathed. This was not the case. There were plenty of times that it hurt. There were also plenty of times when it seemed like I was losing the fight. When I had battles to fight, however, I knew I always had the support of my family and friends. For me, breaking barriers is a process of taking an ending and turning it into a beginning.

One of the places I have run into problems is in the realm of employment. I work with people with disabilities. I started out in a recreational setting, but eventually I moved into the public schools and began working as an instructional aide. I am currently doing this part-time while attending graduate school in psychology at the University of San Francisco. I intend one day to practice therapy with autistic children.

One obstacle I encountered in my work life occured when I began working with disabled people. I started out as an aide, along with several other new employees, but over the course of the next year-and-a-half everyone else that had started out with me in the department had been promoted. I was the only one who was still an aide, and I wound up quitting eighteen months after starting the job.

I was harassed regularly by my supervisor from the day I started until the day I left. As time went on it became increasingly apparent to me that all this person saw when he looked at me was my own disability. After months of trying to prove myself and make the situation more tolerable, things finally came to a head and I had an all-out confrontation with the supervisor. Unfortunately, at this point I felt I had to involve a lawyer, but two weeks later I resigned and began working at a job that paid twice as much. In this instance, the barrier had proved unyielding, so I went around it.

Another time I ran into problems was when I worked in the school district. I was employed at a local junior high school, and I had been working there for about three months when the following incident occurred.

A student with whom I had been working was starting to do much better on his own, and a new student was just coming into the program. I was assigned to work with the new student, but when I talked with his teachers about my disability they began treating me differently. One of the teachers stopped speaking to me altogether. Another asked me the second day of class to switch with one of my coworkers because he did not know how I would be able to work with the student.

I called the district office and requested a transfer to a nearby elementary school. Next I asked for a meeting with the four teachers involved. I had enlisted the support of my supervisor and the vice principal, and I confronted the teachers, letting them know how it felt when they reacted so strongly and negatively to my disability. They all apologized to me, and ultimately they asked me to stay. I had already requested the transfer, however. Perhaps I acted a bit hastily, opting out of the situation before I gave things a chance to resolve themselves. As far as I was concerned, though, discussing the matter and receiving an apology from the teachers effectively broke down the barrier between us. In the end, I did what I felt was right for me by moving on to the elementary school.

The barriers I confront in life are made up of assumptions, misconceptions, ignorance, and fear. We cannot always quell these fears just by talking about them and questioning their validity, but we can try. I feel barriers come down a lot more easily if you can find a way to work with the people who are imposing them. There are times, though, when this isn't possible. Then you have no choice but to circumvent the problem or simply smash right through it.

I try to keep in mind that when people react differently to me than to others, it is because I am unique. When confronted with an obstacle in life I try to remind myself, "Yes, I am different. Let me show them that is okay." This catalyzes the process of beginning. Although I don't always like them, it is ultimately the controversies that allow me to progress in life.

In my experience, discrimination disappears a lot more quickly when I am able to work directly with the person on the other side of the barrier. Certainly, discrimination hurts, and it can stand in a person's way as much as any physical limitation. But it can also be an opportunity to say, "Look. I'm not really so different. I see, just in a different way."

AUTOBIOGRAPHY
(with apologies to Nazim Hikmet)
by Desire Vail

I was born in 1932
I lived at my birthplace for twenty-two years
I could hardly wait to get away
at twenty-two I married an Episcopal priest
at forty-one I married a drinking alcoholic
at fifty-two I married a dirty old man
and I've been a poet since I was fifty
some people know all about men some about love
    I know anger
some people know great poems by heart
    I recite mistakes in my judgment
I have borne two sons who are good to me
I've never known real hunger and there are many foods
    I haven't tasted although I've tasted many
at thirty-seven I returned to graduate school
    to learn how to make a living
at twenty-two I typed for the Navy in Washington, D.C.
at thirty-nine I started my first job as a rehab counselor
at forty-eight I flew in four planes with my guide dog
    from Buffalo to South Dakota to ski
I never saw Roosevelt
    although I was born in the Depression
now I benefit from his legacy
my parents tried to make me a Republican
    it didn't work
yet I was late to let my family idols fall
in '66 I nearly committed suicide

in '67 I began a five-year-plan
    to improve my life
I am not a jealous person
I didn't envy Marilyn Monroe one bit
I was never unfaithful to any husband
I'd like to say I never talked behind my friends' backs
    but I probably did
I drink moderately I like the flavor and feeling
I have never earned my keep
    although I've tried
I've white-lied to protect myself and others
I've omitted to tell the whole truth for the same reason
but I'm a truthful person
I've lived in suburban houses city apartments a duplex
    a railroad flat and now in a country log home
    some people are homeless
I went to the Met Carnegie Hall and Broadway shows
    some people haven't heard of these
and for fifteen years didn't go to the places
    most people visit
    churches temples synagogues mosques astrologers
but I've thought a lot about the meaning of life
my poems are published in two chapbooks
    that I can't show my mother
arthritis arrhythmia and hypothyroidism are working on
me
    and I'm blind
I'll never be a great poet or anything like that
but I would like to be

I think I've never been in love

in short
even if today in Bath I am trying
I can say my life was a soap opera
and who knows how long I will live

and what else will happen to me

— Written in Bath, New York, on June 7, 1996

Desire Vail lives in the foothills of the Allegheny Mountains near Bath, New York. Her poems have appeared in two chapbooks, "See How Wet the Street Sounds" and "First Shine of Dawn," as well as in many little magzines, including Acorn Whistle, Blueline, Rosebud, Black River Review, Blue Unicorn, Kaleidoscope and others.

SEEN THROUGH EXPERIENCE

by Jeffrey Friedlander

I was born in Fall River, Massachusetts, on April 13, 1948. My blindness was caused by being placed in an incubator with too much oxygen. To this day, I have light perception in my right eye, but I could never see out of my left eye at all. People often wonder how I have managed to get through life never having been able to see.

At age three-and-a-half I attended what was then the Boston Nursery for Blind Babies, but I was thrown out after two years for throwing temper tantrums and destroying things. It was not clear where I would go next. One alternative was for me to attend the public school near my home, but nobody knew how the teachers would deal with my blindness. The Massachusetts Commission for the Blind recommended that I attend the Walter E. Fernald School, a state institution for the mentally retarded.

Fernald had a special building known as the Greene Blind Unit. I remember crying the first several nights I was there, wanting to go back to my mom and dad. I had previously gotten into the habit of taking wallpaper and plaster off the walls at my parents' home in Fall River. At Fernald I behaved like a "rotten schmuck" from the get-go, taking people's shoes off and removing screws from cabinets, chairs, tables, and light switches. I got the whippings and scoldings I probably deserved at school.

When I was six my parents moved to Newport, Rhode Island, but because of Fernald's residency requirements they retained their legal residence in Fall River. During my ten-year stay at Fernald I learned to read and write Braille, how to type, sing, wash, shave, dress, dust, mop, and take care of low-functioning people. I received mobility instruction and I was taught how to make rugs and belts, presumably to help me develop a vocation.

I was allowed to go home and spend time with my family during Christmas and summer vacations. During my last two years I started going home on selected weekends as well, such as Easter and Thanksgiving. During summer vacations, I used to like to go to the beach, and I would go with my family to visit friends and relatives in Rhode Island and Massachusetts.

In July of 1962, while still at Fernald, I took an achievement test at the Perkins School for the Blind to see where I stood. By that time I had advanced to the level of eighth-grade spelling and science, seventh-grade reading and, sixth-grade arithmetic. Unbeknownst to me, Perkins placed me on their waiting list, and two years later I was asked back for an interview. In August of 1964 the school called my mother to inform her I had been accepted at Perkins.

Shortly thereafter I received my cottage assignment in the mail, and I arrived at school on September 20th. Once settled in, I needed to figure out where everything was. I had to learn how to get to the main building from the cottage, and how to get around the cottage itself. I started off in an ungraded class, where we learned various policies and procedures. I soon advanced to the point where I was only three or four years behind my age level academically, a big improvement from where I had been just a few years earlier.

I took English every year at Perkins, as well as civics, math, science, U.S. history, French, problems of democracy, personal health, and first aid. In the non-academic program I took gym, woodwork, metalwork, caning, weaving, ceramics, and crafts. I also participated in the chorus and glee club. Each year I passed all my requirements, and I did not have to stay back or take any post-graduate courses.

June 12, 1970, was graduation day for me and twenty-seven other blind classmates.

During my years at Perkins I made several trips to Washington, D.C., with the chorus. In 1966 we participated in the Anne Sullivan Centennial, and in 1968 we sang at Helen Keller's funeral. In 1970 the entire senior class took a four-day trip there just before Easter, and we had the opportunity to visit several historic places. I was also able to travel quite a bit with the glee club. We performed in New York, Philadelphia, and Pittsburgh. I loved these trips, and I hated to leave Perkins when the time came.

Not that my experiences at Perkins were universally good, mind you. I vividly recall an episode that occurred in May of 1966. I wanted to get a haircut, but it seemed like I was being asked to wait forever to go to a barbershop. Finally, I decided I couldn't wait any longer, so I began clipping away at my hair with my fingernail clippers. I had been twisting and clipping for something like five hours when the housemaster walked in, saw what I was doing, and whacked me on the head.

"Stop cutting, Jeffrey," he admonished me. "Don't you realize it looks hideous?"

"No," I insisted. "I'm going to finish it."

"No, you're not," he said, taking the clippers away. "You're only going to make it worse."

When I went into the dining room that evening, my French teacher smacked her lips and said, "Oh, my, Jeffrey, it looks awful. What have you done, Jeffrey Friedlander?"

"I clipped my hair with a nail clipper," I told her.

"Why?" she asked incredulously.

"Because I didn't have any money to pay for a haircut and there was nobody to take me into town," I explained.

"Well," she replied, "you should have asked me."

I was placed on room restriction during afternoon and evening hours for the coming week. After chapel the next day, I went up to the headmaster and told him what I had done. He told me he would let it go this time, but if it happened again I might get suspended. I wound up going to the barber on Thursday that week. By the time I was through I looked like Yul Brynner.

After my father died in 1963, my mother sold the house in Newport and moved to Cranston, just south of Providence. The year I started at Perkins, my grandmother came to live with her there. For a portion of each summer until my grandmother died I attended the Beacon Lodge Camp for the Blind in Mount Union, Pennsylvania. I always looked forward to going there and meeting blind people who were older than me, and I hated when it was time to go back home.

In 1970 I was sent to the Industrial Home for the Blind in Brooklyn. I resented the praise I got from the counselors and the instructors there because I knew I was not doing well at all. Mobility training was about the only thing I really benefitted from. But despite the poor conditions of the residences and the lousy neighborhood, I liked it there. I thought it beat Providence hands down. It was a welcome change of scenery.

On St. Patrick's Day 1971, less than two weeks after I left the Industrial Home, I was admitted to the Protestant Guild for the Blind in Rowley, Massachusetts. The truth of the matter is I did not really want to go there, mainly because I wasn't anxious to return to the Boston area. Once accepted, though, I decided to make the most of it. I learned how to write business letters, how to travel by bus and subway, and I made a number of friends among the Guild staff and their clients.

I wasn't particularly happy when in early 1972, the Guild decided to move to a convent located on the side of a hill. The hill was treacherous as we all got out in the winter, and I almost broke my spinal cord falling on a patch of ice one day. Luckily I was able to cushion the fall with my hand.

While the Guild was busy moving, I began taking a correspondence course in Braille proofreading, conducted by the Library of Congress and the National Library Service for the Blind. During my last year-and-a-half at the Guild, I worked for the National Braille Press as a proofreader.

Unfortunately, a policy change was instituted, stipulating that in order to continue working at the National Braille Press I would have to be certified by the Library of Congress. My options were to switch to collating and fact-checking, get certified, or be let go. I was already unhappy with the housing conditions at the Guild, and this policy change proved to be the straw that broke the camel's back. I left the Guild and resigned from my position with the National Braille Press in November, 1973.

I stayed with my mother and grandmother for a month before moving to the Kagan Home for the Blind in Chicago. In 1969 I had begun transcribing books for the Perkins School, and later the Jewish Braille Institute. I resumed this work at the Kagan Home, where I also began transcribing books for individual clients. This helped me keep in practice as I moved toward my proofreading certification. I obtained the necessary study materials from the Library of Congress, and finally, after three tries, I was certified on September 9, 1975.

Six months after I earned my certification, I called the Hadley School in Massachusetts to see if they needed a proofreader. I began doing medical transcription for them, and took courses from them to increase my vocabulary. During this period I started proofreading for Braille, Inc., in Falmouth, Massachusetts, and in time I picked up freelance proofreading work with three or four other agencies.

In order to keep my fingers in the pie, I did a great deal of proofreading on a voluntary basis (something I am doing more and more of these days). I was receiving public assistance while living in Chicago, even though I was working. Because I was receiving aid, I could not have a bank account in my name. Any gift money I received had to be spent down to the last dime. I started taking mobility training in Chicago. I would walk around the block, and in time I learned to get around pretty well. My goal was to be able to get to the dentist on my own. Then, in May of 1975, I was suddenly dropped from public assistance. It's hard to describe how I felt right then. My mother was on her way out to see me, and I felt humiliated telling her what had happened.

I became depressed, and it just seemed to get worse and worse. I finally told a lady friend I had met at the Kagan Home, as well as a volunteer I worked with, that I was at a point where I did not want to live anymore. I felt like I just wanted to walk out onto the street and let myself get run over. I decided to go to the Home's director to see if arrangements could be made for me to have a psychological evaluation, rather than take my depression out on myself and others. The director arranged for the evaluation, and I proved to be of sound mind, and in time I dug myself out from under my depression. This was in 1980.

One thing that helped was meeting some neighbors around the block, people I still keep in touch with. I started learning the routes of the Chicago Transit Authority buses and trains from a blind fellow who works for the CTA, and I practiced getting to various other places on my own in the course of that year. In 1985 my lady friend at Kagan had to move into a nursing home. For the last two-and-a-half years I lived in Chicago, I went to visit her there every weekend no matter what the weather, until her death in 1987.

After hanging around North Park College for several months, I was advised to go up to Evanston to take the SAT at the Educational Testing Service. I got there using two buses and a train, and I did better on the test than I expected. I feel I accomplished more on my own in Chicago than I might have if I had never been dropped from public assistance.

During the early 1980s I had written several letters to the Clovernook Center in Cincinnati applying for work as a proofreader and a bookbinder, but after two years of sending letters without a reply I stopped writing. I started taking training in office skills from the Chicago Lighthouse and pretty much forgot about Clovernook. It was over a year later, in December of 1984, that I received a phone call from Clovernook asking if I was still interested in coming down to work in their bindery. "Yes," I replied. "I'm still interested."

They told me they would be able to take me some time the next year, but they didn't say exactly when. When I finally got the go-ahead, I only had two weeks to pack up my life and move. I'd hoped I would have the chance to go to Cincinnati and look the place over so that I could dispose of stuff I no longer needed. As things worked out, I was given notice on May 3rd that I needed to be at Clovernook by the 20th. Unfortunately, I wasn't able to finish my sorting on such short notice, so a thousand pounds of my belongings were sent Cincinnati, much of which had to be disposed of when I finally got settled. But my bookcase, which I did want to have with me, never made it there at all.

I worked in the bindery when I first got to Clovernook, all the while continuing to study proofreading. In order to work as a proofreader, I had to pass certain tests. I failed on my first three tries, but finally, on the fourth try I passed, and I started work as a proofreader on March 31, 1986. I stayed off Social Security altogether for several years, although these days I do receive some public assistance.

In January of 1997, as I was crossing the street to catch my bus for work, I was struck by a pickup truck. I held onto the body of the vehicle for dear life to keep from getting run over. When the truck finally came to a stop, a traffic cop who was on the scene gave me a ticket for jaywalking, even though I had my white cane with me. Rather than argue with him, I asked him what my fine was, and then accepted his offer of a ride to work.

As the day wore on I found that I couldn't walk well at all. I was taken to the hospital, where I was in the emergency room for ten hours. X-rays showed that I had a fractured tailbone, which was no big surprise to me. I stayed in the hospital for two days, but I had to be in a wheelchair for two weeks. During that time, I underwent therapy three times a week. A nurse would check the swelling in my ankles, and I was put through all kinds of exercises in order to get my strength back. After another set of X-rays at the chiropractor's office, I was told I had to remain out of work for another couple of weeks. Eventually I did not need therapy and nursing, although I had to use the crutches for quite a while.

I had resolved to pay the jaywalking ticket, but before I did so I was informed that I had the right of way when the truck hit me. In February 1998, I appeared in traffic court to argue my case, and the charges were dropped. The driver of the pickup apologized profusely for what had happened, although not to me directly. I decided not to sue because I had no desire to go through the paperwork. Besides, no amount of money was going to make me feel any better. As long as I had enough money in the bank, what more did I want? All I really wanted was to get my life back together.

In April 1998, buzzers were installed at Race and Vine Streets on 15th, the block where the accident had occurred. To me, this is very gratifying, and I remain undeterred. I did, however, have to participate in a thorough review of that part of Cincinnati.

At present I am a life member of four organizations: the Braille Revival League, the National Braille Association, Educators of the Visually Handicapped, and the Association of California Transcribers. I am also an active member of the Perkins Alumni Association. I've had a long and active life, and on the whole, it has been good to me.

AFTERWORD

A BRIEF HISTORY OF BLINDNESS

From the Dark Ages to modern times, the barriers experienced by blind people can be traced, following a pattern of: 1) separation from the community; 2) transition into the community; and finally 3) integration into sighted society. Some ancient civilizations separated the blind from "healthy" members of society. It was not uncommon for babies with blindness or other "defects" to be put out to sea in wicker baskets to starve or drown, or left on mountaintops to freeze and die. In the Middle Ages, blind people usually had little choice but to be beggars, making them objects of scorn, ridicule and ribald amusement. Groups of blind men wandered the countryside making fools of themselves in order to earn their daily bread, holding onto each other for support as they stumbled along.

Centuries passed before the plight of the blind touched the conscience of either the church or the state. Then the blind were harbored in monasteries, put to work on farms, or assigned special places on church steps for begging. Finally, they became wards of the state. Self-respect and the respect of others was negligible. Not until the eighteenth century did the accomplishments of individual blind people start to be widely recognized. Starting around this time they became musicians, mathematicians and philosophers, but their recognition was always on an individual basis.

Dante's Divine Comedy speaks of blindness. Breugel, who painted seventeenth-century peasant scenes, included blind people in his paintings. His eye was so keen that one can discern the specific diseases of each blind person he depicted. Homer was blind; Milton was blind; Handel and Bach suffered as well. Francois Huber, a blind Swiss naturalist, produced a definitive study of bees. All of these visually impaired people made valuable contributions to the broader society, and their individual emancipations eventually led to integration into the sighted world.

By the nineteenth century, schools for the blind had been established in Scotland and France. The most famous Parisian student was Louis Braille. When Braille was three years old, he became blind through an accident in his father's shop. He was sent to a school for the blind in Paris, where he invented a reading system of raised dots. Braille based his system on a raised-dot code used by a French general to send messages to his troops at night. Braille's system broke the barriers of blind illiteracy, enabling blind people to read with their fingers what others read with their eyes. Today this system is used all over the world in a multitude of languages.

Modern opportunities for employment have increased through new technologies. There are blind telephone operators and blind typists. Blind people operate newsstands. In this country the government has provided opportunities for the blind to manage public cafeterias and to sell real estate and insurance. Gone are the days of sheltered workshops for the blind; now high schools, colleges and extended education centers offer courses in computer literacy.

In this century in the United States, the mainstreaming of blind children from sheltered schools into the general school population has become common practice. Specially trained resource teachers help blind students keep abreast of their studies. Itinerant teachers visit the homes of children who can't get to a central school. Braille literacy is emphasized. Talking book libraries offer recreational and scholarly studies. Audio descriptions in theaters and movies, as well as on television, extend opportunities for the visually impaired.

The blind community is enjoying more freedom—personal, social, political, and legal—than ever before; at home, in school, in the workplace and in society. The Americans With Disabilities Act addresses the requirements of people who do in fact have special needs.

The world of electronics has been a great equalizer. Talking computers turn out typewritten documents. Computers translate spoken words into Braille and translate Braille into print. State Departments of Rehabilitation teach Braille, as well as orientation and mobility skills (learning one's place in space). They teach everyday living skills, offer employment opportunities, and provide school placement. These are all ways in which barriers against the blind are being broken.

THE DICK AND JANE PRIMER OF COMMON EYE DISORDERS

The American Academy of Opthalmology says low vision is when "ordinary eye glasses or contact lenses are unable to bring a person's sight up to normal."

DEFINITIONS

This section contains simple descriptions of a few conditions that can cause loss of vision or blindness. Here are some medical words that need some explanation:

Opthalmologist - A doctor who treats the eye and is an eye surgeon.

Optometrist - A person trained to examine eyes and prescribe glasses. Although optometrists often test for eye diseases, they are not trained to treat them.

Optician - A person who makes glasses.

Optical Aids - Things you can use to help you see better, like eyeglasses, magnifying lenses, and other kinds of enlargers.

Laser - A powerful beam of light that can sometimes be used to cut or seal tissue without surgery.

Peripheral Vision - Vision to the left, right, above, and below what you are looking at.

Cornea - The thin clear tissue that is the front of the eyeball.

Vitreous - The clear gel inside the eyeball. It keeps the eyeball's shape and allows light to pass through.

Pupil - The black spot in the center of the eyeball. It is actually a hole, covered by the cornea, through which light passes.

Iris - The colored circle around the pupil that changes

the size of the pupil for different light conditions.

Lens - The lens is just behind the pupil. It focuses what you see on the retina at the back of the eye.

Retina - A nerve tissue in the back of the eye. It catches the light that has passed through the lens and sends it on to the brain, where it becomes pictures.

Macula - The macula is in the center of the retina. It gives us forward vision, allowing us to read and to see exactly what things look like.

Optic Nerve - The optic nerve connects the retina to the brain. It is the path along which the light captured by the retina travels to the brain.

COMMON EYE DISORDERS

Cataracts

Condition - A cataract is like a clouding of the lens of the eye. When the lens is clear, it passes light to the retina. Sometimes the clouding continues for a long time before you know your sight is changing. A cataract can cause hazy or foggy vision. The pupil, which is normally black, can turn yellowish or cloudy white.

Cause - There are many kinds of cataracts. The most common is the kind that develops as we grow older, starting at about age forty. This is called a senile cataract.

Sometimes babies are are born with cataracts. This kind of cataract is called a congenital cataract. When these cataracts are treated immediately, the baby's sight can be saved. Neglect can lead to blindness.

Another kind of cataract can result from an injury to the eye, such as poking, hitting, or cutting. This is called a traumatic cataract.

Sometimes other diseases, like diabetes, can start a cataract. This is called a secondary cataract.

Care - So far, the only thing that can cure a cataract is

surgery. Ask your opthalmologist about medicine, eye drops, or other treatments that you think might be helpful.

Cure - Almost all cataract operations are successful, but there is always a risk with any surgery. In cataract surgery the cloudy lens is taken out.

Once the lens is removed, your eye needs a substitute lens. This could be special cataract glasses, contact lenses, or permanent artificial lenses put in the eye.

Sometimes it takes a long time for good sight to return. Talk to your opthalmologist about the best method for you.

For safety's sake, it can never hurt to keep your head above your heart after eye surgery. Avoid bending over after eye surgery until your opthalmologist says your eye has completely healed.

Macular Degeneration

Condition - Macular degeneration is a breakdown of sight in the retina. The macula is part of the retina. You might notice a dark or empty spot when you look at something. Sometimes, if macular degeneration happens only in one eye, you don't even know there's a dark or empty spot because the other eye is doing the work of two eyes.

Cause - Most of the time, macular degeneration is caused by a thinning or breakdown of the retina around the macula. Sometimes the blood vessels break down and scar tissue blocks your sight.

Care and Coping - As the macula becomes weaker or degenerates, you will find reading and close-up work more difficult. The way you perceive colors may change. When you feel your sight is changing, the best thing to do is visit your opthalmologist right away.

You may find different ways to make it easier to see, such as magnifying glasses and brighter lights. Your library may have machines that magnify what you wish to read.

Most have large-print and "talking" books. Ask the librarian about other things they may have for low-vision people.

Cure - There is no cure for macular degeneration. In a few cases, early in the disorder, laser surgery may help. It is important to visit your opthalmologist right away when you notice a change in your sight.

Glaucoma

Condition - At first, glaucoma affects your vision above, below, and to the sides of what you are looking at (your peripheral vision). Glaucoma may give you tunnel vision, where you can see straight ahead, but not to the left or right or up or down.

Fluid pressure builds up in the eye and causes pressure against the nerves. This happens because the fluid inside the eyeball can't drain out of the eye. The drain in the eye is called a canal. Imagine a washcloth blocking the drain of your bathtub, and the water staying in the tub and not being able to drain out. That is what it is like when the canal of your eye is blocked and the fluid cannot drain. The pressure from the fluid damages the optic nerve. The nerve is important because it connects the eye to the brain. Glaucoma is usually slow and painless and is sometimes called "the silent enemy."

Cause - Most of the time glaucoma happens because the drainage canals are blocked. Usually the block is mild. The fluid drains out more slowly and your eyesight changes very slowly. Sometimes the canal is blocked very suddenly and the pressure builds up very quickly. Then you might feel pain or become nauseated and your sight will be blurred. You might even become blind in a day. Put in an emergency call to your public clinic or opthalmologist right away.

Care - Glaucoma can generally be treated if found in the

early stages. It does not usually lead to blindness. Eye drops and/or pills are usually used to treat glaucoma. If you have side effects from the medicine, tell your opthalmologist. Sometimes laser treatments can be used to reduce the pressure in the eye. Surgery is sometimes able to create new drainage openings.

As with macular degeneration, try to keep your head above your heart after glaucoma surgery. Avoid bending over until your opthalmologist says your eye has completely healed.

Cure - There is no cure for glaucoma. Treatment can keep the disorder under control and prevent most loss of sight, but the best cure is prevention, and the best prevention is eye exams. The common rule is to have an eye exam once a year after age forty.

Diabetic Retinopathy

Condition - Diabetic retinopathy is a combination of two words. It means that a person with diabetes may have a disorder in the retina. Diabetes affects blood sugar levels. Blood sugar levels affect the blood vessels in the retina. The blood vessels change size and sometimes leak.

Cause - The exact cause of diabetic retinopathy is not understood. Diabetes, however, seems to cause a weakening of the capillaries (very small blood vessels) all over the body. Pregnancy or high blood pressure often make this condition worse.

There are two types of diabetic retinopathy. In background retinopathy the blood vessels within the retina change. This is an early stage of diabetic retinopathy. Sight is usually not seriously affected and the disorder does not get worse in about 80% of diabetic people with the disorder. However, the abnormal blood vessels may leak fluid and protein into the macula, the area that subserves central vision, causing what is known as diabetic macular edema.

Patients with this condition may notice a decrease in their central or reading vision.

A second, more advanced form of retinopathy is called proliferative retinopathy. This begins the same way as background retinopathy. The fragile new blood vessels break and bleed into the vitreous (the clear fluid in the eye). This blood causes the fluid to become cloudy, which blurs vision. Also, scar tissue forms, which tightens and pulls on the retina. This may pull the retina away from the tissue behind it (retinal detachment).

Blood vessels may also form abnormally in the iris, which can cause a type of glaucoma. Blindness may result from these conditions.

Care and Coping - Sometimes treatment for diabetic retinopathy is not necessary, especially with background retinopathy where vision is not affected. Only your opthalmologist can tell. Other times, however, eye treatment is necessary to stop the disorder or improve vision. A very important treatment is "laser treatment." This means a surgeon directs a short burst of light that seals leaking blood vessels and forms small scars. These small scars reduce the abnormal vessel growth and help connect or attach the retina back to the eye. Laser treatment may help stop the damage, even in advanced cases. Remember, this method may not help you. It depends on the size and location of the damage, and how much the vitreous is clouded with blood. In some cases, other surgery might help. A surgical procedure called a vitrectomy removes the vitreous and replaces it with an artificial clear solution. About 70% of vitrectomy patients have improved sight.

Again, try to keep your head above your heart after surgery and avoid bending over until your opthalmologist says your eye has completely healed.

Cure - There is no cure for diabetes or diabetic retinopathy. Studies have shown that keeping diabetes under tight control significantly reduces the chance of losing vision.

Successful treatment depends upon early diagnosis, taking all prescribed medications, and following the self-care recommended by your opthalmologist.

Retinosis Pigmentosa

Condition - Retinitis pigmentosa is a hereditary disease that affects vision. It is usually first detected by patients in childhood. The earliest symptoms are inability to see in the dark and loss of peripheral vision.

Cause - Retinitis pigmentosa is caused by abnormal cells in the retina. Retinitis pigmentosa means a darker color in the cells within the retina. Males have this disorder more often than females. The disorder develops slowly over the course of years, and often does not lead to very low vision since central vision is the last to be affected. Sometimes people with this condition are able to see well for most of their lives. Others, however, may go blind.

Care and Coping - There is no treatment known to stop retinitis pigmentosa. Many aids are available to improve vision affected by retinitis pigmentosa. Some of these include special lenses to expand peripheral vision. Other mechanical and electronic devices may also work for some people. Ask your opthalmologist or clinic for information.

Cure - There is no cure for retinitis pigmentosa.

****

OTHER CONDITIONS THAT APPEAR IN THIS BOOK

Nystagmus: Functional defect. Involuntary, rhythmic side-to-side, or up and down (oscillating) eye movements that are faster in one direction than another.

Cystoid Macular Edema: (CME, degeneration from) Pathologic condition. Retinal swelling and cyst formation in macular area; usually results in temporary decrease in vision, though it may be permanent. Frequently occurs to some extent after cataract surgery; specific cause unknown.

Ulcer, Corneal Ulcer: Pathologic condition. Area of epithelial tissue loss from corneal surface; associated with inflammatory cells in the cornea and anterior chamber. Usually caused by a bacterial, fungal, or viral infection.

PHPV: (persistent hyperplastic primary vitreous) Chronic increased number of cone type of cells. Increased frequency of cell division.

Retinoblastoma: Pathologic condition. Hereditary, malignant intraocular tumor that develops from retinal pigment cells. Untreated, numerous seeding nodule producing secondary tumors, gradually filling the eye and extending along the optic nerve to the brain, causing death. Most common as childhood (infant) ocular malignancy.

Abnormal Cell Development of the Primary Vitreous: Pathologic condition. Abnormal development of the vitreous, the transparent, colorless gelatinous mass that fills the rear two-thirds of the interior of the eyeball.

Hemonymous Hemianopsia: Functional defect. Defect in the right or left half of the visual field.

Retrolental Fibroplasia: (RLF, retinopathy of prematurity) Pathologic condition. Series of retinal changes that sometimes develops after life-sustaining oxygen therapy is given to premature infants. Sometimes regresses. Other complications include glaucoma, cataract, nearsightedness, sunken eyes, eye misalignment.

Lieber's Optic Atrophy: Pathologic condition. Optic nerve

degeneration characterized by optic disc paleness; usually results in irreversible loss of vision.

Hyperthyroidism: Pathologic condition. Neuromuscular changes, increased metabolism caused by excessive thyroid hormone concentration. Symptoms include fatigue, weight loss, tremors, sweating, rise in blood pressure. Eye: lid lag, lid retraction, strabismus. (Grave's, Basedow's, etc.).

Multiple Sclerosis: Pathologic condition. Chronic central nervous system disorder in which there is loss of the protective myelin sheath surrounding nerve tissue. Eye findings include optic nerve inflammation with reduced vision, double vision, and involuntary eye oscillations (nystagmus).